KAREN ARMSTRONG

Sacred Nature

How We Can Recover Our Bond with the Natural World

VINTAGE

1 3 5 7 9 10 8 6 4 2

Vintage is part of the Penguin Random House group of companies
whose addresses can be found at global.penguinrandomhouse.com

First published in Vintage in 2023
First published in hardback by The Bodley Head in 2022

penguin.co.uk/vintage

Printed and bound in Great Britain by Clays Ltd, Elcograf S.p.A.

The authorised representative in the EEA is Penguin Random House
Ireland, Morrison Chambers, 32 Nassau Street, Dublin D02 YH68

A CIP catalogue record for this book is available from the British Library

ISBN 9781529114799

Penguin Random House is committed to a sustainable future for
our business, our readers and our planet. This book is made from
Forest Stewardship Council® certified paper.

In Memoriam

Felicity Bryan
(16 October 1945–21 June 2020)

Contents

Heaven is my father and Earth is my mother
and even such a small creature as I finds
an intimate place in their midst.

Therefore that which fills the universe
I regard as my body
and that which directs the universe
I consider as my nature.

All people are my brothers and sisters, and
all the things [in nature] are my companions.

From the 'Western Inscription'
(*Ximing*) by Zhang Zai

Introduction

I vividly remember my first visit to the British Museum, a place that has since become so familiar and important to me. I was a young nun, studying for university entrance, and my tutor had told me to go and look at the manuscripts on display. In those days, the British Library was housed in the museum, and I found myself gazing in wonder at the handwriting of Wordsworth, Coleridge and Keats. The immediacy of their presence was almost shocking; time seemed to have collapsed. I was looking at the moment that these poems, which were now a part of myself, had come into being. I did not want to analyse the manuscripts. I simply wanted to be in their presence. It was a kind of communion.

My reaction may sound extreme, but I was not a typical museum visitor. For over four years I had lived in a convent entirely cut off from the outside world. We heard no news. As an exception, we were informed about the Cuban Missile Crisis of 1962, but our superiors forgot to tell us when it was over, so we spent three weeks waiting anxiously for Armageddon. For four years, I had seen no television, no films, no newspapers. I had no idea about the social revolution of the sixties. As I contemplated the manuscripts, shrouded in my all-enveloping religious habit, I was more like a closeted Victorian girl than a young woman of the mid twentieth century.

Today, when I watch visitors to the museum encountering the great relics of the past, I notice that they seem impelled not just to look but to take photographs. Unlike my younger self, they do not seem to want simply to commune with the Rosetta Stone, for example, but to seek to own it in some way, as though it does not become real to them until they have a virtual copy. Do the changes I have seen over sixty years in even such a small act of witnessing not reflect our changed relationship with nature? We walk in a place of extreme beauty while talking on our mobiles or scrolling through social media: we are present, yet fundamentally absent. Instead of sitting contemplatively beside a river or gazing in awe at a mountain range, we obsessively take one photograph of the view after another. Rather than let the landscape find an intimate place in our minds and hearts, we are distancing ourselves from nature, which is becoming a simulated reality. Our urban living and all-absorbing technology have alienated us from nature, so that even the magnificent films of David Attenborough may fail to reach our innermost core.

Some of us strongly feel that sense of alienation and loss. But it is not a recent phenomenon. The Romantic poets whose manuscripts in the British Library filled me with such wonder had already mourned our broken relationship with nature. William Wordsworth (1770–1850) recalled the luminous vision of the world that he had enjoyed as a boy but lost as a grown-up:

There was a time when meadow, grove
and stream,
The earth, and every common sight,
To me did seem
Apparelled in celestial light,
The glory and the freshness of a dream.
It is not now as it hath been of yore.
Turn wheresoe'er I may.
By night or day
The things that I have seen I now can see no more.

He is still aware of the beauty of nature but knows 'there hath passed away a glory from the earth'. He sees a tree and a field that both 'speak of something that hath gone'.

> Whither is fled the visionary gleam?
> Where is it now the glory and the dream?

In my own humble way, I recall something similar. I grew up in the unspoilt Worcestershire countryside in the late 1940s and distinctly remember trying to tell my puzzled parents about something I called 'putsch'. There was no word I knew of for what I recall as a strange but compelling luminosity in the woods and lanes near our home that I could not make my adult companions see. They assumed I was thinking of the fairies pictured in my story books, but it was more of an impersonal, all-encompassing radiance. Once I went to school to be inducted into the rational worldview that governs modern life, I, like Wordsworth, experienced the 'light and glory die away, / And fade into the light of common day'.

But our changed relationship with nature is not just an aesthetic loss. Over many years now, we have become increasingly aware of the damage we are inflicting on the natural environment and its potentially drastic impact on human life. It is true that the earth's climate has continually altered over the millennia, but hitherto this has always been a slow process, and we are now seeing rapid changes. Global temperatures and sea levels are rising at an alarming rate and this is entirely due to human activity. We know that burning fossil fuels releases carbon dioxide into the earth's atmosphere, where it is trapped and causes the earth's temperature to rise. Unless this is checked, human life will be imperilled. Water shortages will make it increasingly hard to produce food. Some regions will become dangerously hot, while rising sea levels will make others uninhabitable. Already, polar ice and glaciers are melting fast. Scientists have set a temperature increase of 1.5 degrees centigrade as the 'safe' limit for global warming. If the temperature goes any higher, human life as we know it will be impossible.

As I write this introduction in the summer of 2021, the environmental crisis has assumed new urgency. Temperatures in the United States and southern Europe have reached their highest ever levels, leading to devastating forest fires that have destroyed entire communities. At the same time, Germany and the Netherlands have suffered unprecedented flooding, which has taken lives and wreaked appalling damage. Climate change is no longer an alarming possibility; it has become a fearful reality. Disaster can be averted only if we change the way we live. This crisis has been caused by our modern way of life, which, despite its considerable achievements, is fatally flawed. We are beginning to realise that the way we live now, for all its manifold benefits, not only inhibits human flourishing but threatens the very survival of our species. We have to change not only our lifestyle but our whole belief system. We have ransacked nature, treating it as a mere resource, because over the last 500 years we have cultivated a worldview that is very different from that of our forebears.

* * *

Wordsworth's perception of the sacrality of nature – its 'light and glory' – may resemble the way we perceived the world when humanity was in its infancy. Today this primal way of life has survived only in a few remaining communities of indigenous tribal peoples. When, in the late eighteenth and early nineteenth centuries, the first Western explorers in Australia, Africa and the Americas watched a shaman entering a trance state, they assumed he was experiencing the 'supernatural' or exploring his 'inner world'. But the shaman did not encounter gods, nor was he making an interior spiritual journey. Rather, he was acting as an intermediary between his community and its natural environment, ensuring that there was a fruitful interchange between the two. He had no conception of what we call the supernatural. He was not looking beyond or above nature, nor was he seeking the divine within himself, like a modern contemplative. Instead, the shaman projects his awareness outwards into the depths of the landscape, which for him is alive, spiritually, psychologically and sensuously. He experiences an awareness which he and his community have in common with the animals, insects and plants around them – even with the lichen growing on a stone. Where tribal people sense reciprocity between themselves and the natural environment, we moderns see it as a mere backdrop to human affairs. But before the development of modern Western civilisation, our own ancestors would have shared this primordial understanding.

The American anthropologist David Abram believes that our modern Western focus on the 'inner world' and the Christian idea of a supernatural heaven are both results of a profound psychic change. At an earlier stage of our history, we would have experienced nature as animate too, but over time we have come to regard it as mechanical, prosaic and predictable.[1] After spending many years living intimately with indigenous people of Indonesia and Nepal and studying their cultures, Abram began to understand that they had a far more developed perception of nature than we have in the modern West. What is more, by immersing himself wholly in these tribal cultures, he found that he was starting to develop such insight himself. One night, when sheltering in a cave during a violent rainstorm, he became fascinated watching two spiders weaving an intricate web, creating one elaborate and beautiful pattern after another:

> It was from them that I learned of the intelligence that lurks in nonhuman nature . . . leaving one open to a world all alive, awake and aware. It was from such small beings that my senses first learned of the countless worlds within worlds that spin in the depths of this world that we commonly inhabit, and from them that I learned that my body could, with practice, enter sensorially into these dimensions.[2]

Over the years, he found that he was experiencing hitherto-unexplored levels of consciousness.

When a shaman spoke of a 'power' or 'presence' in the corner of his house, Abram realised that a sunbeam illuminating a column of dust was indeed a power, an active force that not only imbued the air currents with warmth but altered the mood of the room. When walking on dirt paths through the landscape, he learned to slow his pace and become conscious of the spiritual and physical difference between one hill and another.

For most of us, immersed as we are in urban life and increasingly retreating from the world of nature into technology, such an experience is alien. Where we see a range of separate beings and phenomena, tribal people see a continuum of time and space, where animals, plants and humans are all permeated by an immanent sacred force that draws them into a synthesised whole. For millennia, long before the development of urban civilisation, this was probably how most humans experienced the natural world.

The first Western explorers assumed that the 'uncivilised natives' they encountered held these strange beliefs because their brains were insufficiently developed. But the French anthropologist Lucien Lévy-Bruhl (1857–1939) was convinced that they were neurologically identical with our own.[3] When faced with a practical problem, they were able to respond quickly and efficiently, solving it with skill and insight. Their minds were not different from ours, he concluded; they simply relied on different regions of the brain. Modern neurologists would probably agree. They have pointed out that while we in the modern West tend to rely more on the left hemisphere of the brain, the home of rational and pragmatic thought, tribal people have a right-hemispheric worldview, which identifies connection between things; indeed, the right hemisphere is the source of poetry, music, art and religion. Lévy-Bruhl used the term 'participation' to describe the logic of indigenous people, who experience not just humans and animals but apparently 'inanimate' objects, such as stones and plants, as having a life of their own, each participating in the same mode of existence and influencing each other.

The essence of this 'participatory' understanding of the natural world did not die with the arrival of civilisation. It would be expressed differently in each culture but, until the advent of Western modernity, it remained substantially similar across the world. We will see that people in early civilisations did not experience the power that governed the cosmos as a supernatural, distant and distinct 'God'. It was rather an intrinsic presence that they, like the nineteenth-century shaman, experienced in ritual and contemplation – a force imbuing all things, a transcendent mystery that could never be defined. In the ancient Middle East, *ilam*, meaning 'divinity' in Akkadian, was a radiant power that transcended any singular deity. In India, the Brahman, the ultimate reality, was indefinable; it was a sacred energy that was deeper, higher and more fundamental than the *devas*, the gods who were present in nature but had no control over the natural order. In China, the ultimate reality was the *Dao*, the fundamental 'Way' of the cosmos; nothing could be said about it, because it transcended all normal categories.

Monotheism, the belief in a single God that is central to the faith of Jews, Christians and Muslims, was the great exception. At the very beginning of the Hebrew Bible, in the first chapter of Genesis, God issues a command to the first human beings, giving them total dominion over the natural world: 'Be fruitful, multiply, fill the earth and conquer it. Be masters of the fish of the sea, the birds of heaven and all living animals on earth.'[4] Unlike the other scriptures we shall consider, the Hebrew Bible does not focus on the sanctity of nature, because the people of Israel experienced the divine in human events rather than in the natural world. The historian of religion Mircea Eliade (1907–86) argued that they were the first people to perceive history as a succession of unique and unrepeatable occurrences.[5] So while the ancient Egyptians regarded the annual flooding of the Nile and the rising and setting of the sun as divine events, the Israelites saw the hand of their god Yahweh in the incidents of their past and the political challenges of the present. However, so deeply embedded was nature's sacrality in the human psyche that some Jews and Christians, in their distinctive ways, would also affirm it. And as we will see, Muslims made it central to their faith.

But in early modern Europe, the link between nature and the divine was severed, and Christians began to see 'God' as separate from the world. Originally, European Christians, like the peoples of the Middle East, India and China, had seen the sacred as a ubiquitous force that pervaded the natural world and pulled the disparate elements of the universe together. As the Dominican theologian Thomas Aquinas (1225–74) had explained in his definitive *Summa Theologiae*, God was not confined to a supernatural heaven but was 'present everywhere in everything'. God was not *a* being but rather 'Being *Itself*' (*esse seipsum*), the divine essence at the heart of all things. God was all that is, Thomas taught, so 'wherever God exists he exists wholly'.[6] But Thomas's theology was to be superseded with a radical shift in the Western conception of the divine. By the fourteenth century, students at the universities of Paris, Oxford and Bologna were studying logic, mathematics and Aristotelian science before they began their theological studies, and when they arrived in divinity school, they were so well versed in logical thought that they instinctively tried to describe theological issues in rational terms. The Franciscan philosopher John Duns Scotus (1265–1308) was one of the first to develop a rational, almost scientific theology. As a result, in Western Christendom, people were beginning to regard God as just another being – albeit of a superior kind – rather than 'Being Itself', and it was not long before they would break with the more traditional understanding of the sacred.

The English philosopher Francis Bacon (1561–1626) went a step further than the medieval rationalists, pioneering an essentially empirical philosophy. By investigating the phenomena of nature carefully and experimentally, he argued, human beings could discover the laws that governed these forces and would then be able to exploit nature for their own benefit. For Bacon, knowledge was power.

God had given Adam clear instructions to 'fill the earth and conquer it', but God's original plan had been foiled by Adam's disobedience. It was now time for philosophers to repair the damage wrought by the Fall and for humans to break with the ingrained – the pagan – habit of revering nature. They must control and subdue the earth as God had commanded. Nature was no longer a theophany, a revelation of the divine; it was a commodity that must be exploited.

Eventually theology and science came to be regarded as different disciplines in Christian Europe: while theology promoted the study of God, science would explore the natural laws that ruled the earth and thus initiate a new era of human power and progress. While Bacon had inspired the energy and direction of the new science, it was the French philosopher René Descartes (1596–1650) who established its theoretical foundation by applying the discipline of mathematics to modern thought. Only through mathematics, he believed, could humans acquire accurate and trustworthy information about the world. A scientist must empty his mind of both divine revelation and human tradition. He must not even trust the evidence derived from his senses, since these too could be deceptive; he might be dreaming when he thought he saw or touched different objects. By laying aside everything he thought he knew the philosopher could achieve a certitude based solely on ideas that were self-evident.

Descartes' famous maxim '*Cogito ergo sum*' ('I think, therefore I am') was, he argued, the only point of certainty, which nothing in the external world could provide. For Descartes, the modern mind had deliberately retreated from nature; it should be solitary, autonomous and a world unto itself, unaffected by and separate from all other beings. And because the material universe was lifeless, godless and inert, nature could tell us nothing about God, the ultimate reality. In Descartes' writings, there is none of the awe that had informed traditional views of the sacred. Indeed, it was the task of science to dispel such reverence. In the future, he believed, people would look at the clouds 'in such a way that we will no longer have occasion to wonder at anything that can be seen of them, or anything that descends from them'.[7] Indeed, the phenomena of nature resembled the new machines that were now appearing in seventeenth-century Europe – clocks, mills and fountains. They had no inner life, and their value was purely utilitarian. The stage was set for nature's exploitation.

Descartes' rational ethos was endorsed by the British physicist and philosopher Isaac Newton (1642–1727). For Newton too, nature no longer had a sacred core; matter, he argued, was lifeless and inert, unable to move or develop unless acted upon by an outside force. In Newton's theology, God was reduced to a physical phenomenon. Picking up on the note of mastery in the Genesis creation story, Newton defined God's essence as *dominatio* ('dominion'), which he identified with the force of gravity that controls the cosmos. The concept of dominion, which would acquire a political edge when Europeans established their empires, would reduce nature to a resource to be exploited. There was no transcendence because this God was simply a larger and more powerful version of the human scientist, 'a voluntary Agent' who was 'very well skilled in Mechanicks and Geometry'.[8] What we call God had been given a clearly defined function in the universe and deemed a rational inference from its intricate design. Newton had no time for awe or mystery. ''Tis the temper of the hot and superstitious part of mankind in matters of religion,' he wrote irritably, 'ever to be fond of mysteries & for that reason to like best what they understand least.'[9] His disciple Samuel Clarke (1675–1729), hailed in his lifetime as the most important theologian in Britain, had a drastically reductive view of both God and nature: 'There is no such thing as what men call the course of nature or the power of nature. [It] is nothing else but the will of God producing certain effects in a continued regular, constant and uniform manner.'[10] It was only a matter of time before scientists would focus on these effects and find the God element unnecessary.

Some of Newton's physics soon became outdated, but his theology has remained influential in Western thought. When people claim today that they do not 'believe' in God, they are usually rejecting Newton's God, the 'Mechanickal' Creator who designed and dominated the universe. But this view of the divine is unique to the modern West. So deeply ingrained is the idea of the sacrality of nature, that even though people throughout the world have embraced Western science and technology, adopted Western forms of government and followed the West by exploiting the natural world, this narrow perception of the divine has never been wholly accepted in other religions. Many non-Western people still do not comprehend the full implications of our secular concept of nature. They believe that Western science may help them to control their affairs more effectively, but they have not always realised what this means for their form of the sacred – or indeed for the future of Planet Earth.[11]

* * *

While it is essential to cut carbon emissions and heed the warnings of scientists, we need to learn not only how to act differently but also how to think differently about the natural world. We need to recover the veneration of nature that human beings carefully cultivated for millennia; if we fail to do this, our concern for the natural environment will remain superficial. But this doesn't have to be an insuperable task, because despite our careless and destructive behaviour, we have not entirely lost our love of nature. Our poets still extol the beauty and mystery of the natural world and David Attenborough's wildlife documentaries continue to attract huge audiences. People flock to the sea for holidays and walk in the woods or in parks at weekends – a return to nature which is both pleasurable and restorative. Even in our large, polluted cities, people cherish their garden, a little oasis of nature in the urban desert. We should consciously develop this remnant of our primordial link to nature in our struggle to save the planet. It is essential not only to our well-being but to our humanity.

This will require imagination and effort. It is crucial that we behave differently not just when we feel like it but all the time. Here the religious practices and disciplines of the past have much to offer. They can help us to develop an aesthetic appreciation of nature and to devise an ethical programme that will guide our behaviour and our thoughts. We must revive the reverence for the natural world that has always been essential to human nature but has become peripheral. Some environmentalists, inspired by tribal peoples' profound relationship with nature, believe that they should be our role models. But this may be too ambitious. Unlike David Abrams, most of us simply cannot live for long years in the wild to imbibe the wisdom and vision of indigenous people. Nor can many of us spend hours every day communing with nature and meditating in the outdoors, as some committed environmentalists do.

But I believe that we can learn a great deal from the insights and practices that developed during the Axial Age (*c.* 900 to 200 BCE), so called because it was pivotal to the spiritual and intellectual development of our species. At that time, in four distinct regions of the world, the great religious and philosophical traditions arose that have nourished humanity ever since: Confucianism and Daoism in

China; Hinduism and Buddhism in India; monotheism in Israel; and rationalism in Greece. Each of these traditions pioneered a new kind of spirituality. Tribal religion, profound though it was, was felt to be no longer relevant in the new and complex civilisations in which many people now lived. These new spiritualities, despite their differences, all shared a common ethos and, crucially, a similar understanding of humanity's relationship with the natural world. We have never wholly surpassed the profound insights of this time. It is not a question of believing religious doctrines; it is about incorporating into our lives insights and practices that will not only help us to meet today's serious challenges but change our hearts and minds.

1

Mythos and Logos

A great deal of environmental discussion is scientific: we constantly hear about emissions, particles, pollution levels and the ozone layer. This provides us with essential information and we have become familiar with the terminology. But it does not move us emotionally. Today we tend to use the term 'myth' rather vaguely to mean something that is not true. When we hear of gods walking on the earth, a dead man striding out of his tomb or a sea parting to release an enslaved people, we dismiss these tales as 'only myths'. But in the past, 'myth' meant something entirely different.

For most of human history, there were two ways of thinking, speaking and acquiring knowledge about the world: *mythos* and *logos*.[1] Both were essential to comprehending reality: they were not in opposition to one another but complementary modes of arriving at truth, and each had its special area of competence. Mythos was concerned with what was considered timeless. It looked both back to the origins of life and culture and inward to the deepest levels of human experience. It was concerned with meaning not practical affairs. Humans are meaning-seeking creatures. If our lives lack significance, we fall very easily into despair, and it was mythos that introduced people to deeper truths, making sense of their moribund and precarious lives by directing their attention to the eternal and universal. As far as we know, cats do not agonise about the feline condition, worry about the plight of cats in other parts of the world, or try to see life from a different perspective. But from a very early period humans felt compelled to devise stories that enabled them to place their lives in a different setting and give them a conviction that – against all the depressing evidence to the contrary – life had some meaning and value.

A myth is an event which, in some sense, happened once, but which also happens all the time. Mythology points beyond the chaotic flux of historical events to what is timeless in human life, helping us to glimpse the stable core of reality. It is also rooted in what we call the unconscious mind. Myths are an ancient form of psychology. When people told tales of heroes descending into the underworld, struggling through labyrinths or fighting with monsters, they were bringing to light fears and desires from the obscure regions of the subconscious mind, which is not accessible by purely logical investigation but has a profound effect on our experience and behaviour. Myth could not be conveyed by rational proof; its insights were intuitive, like those of art and poetry. What's more, myth became a reality only when it was embodied in rituals and ceremonies, enabling participants to apprehend the deeper currents of life. Myth and ritual were so inseparable that it is a matter of scholarly debate which came first. Without spiritual practice, the mythical story would make no sense – in rather the same way as a musical score remains opaque to most of us until it is interpreted instrumentally.

We are far more conversant today with logos, which is quite different from mythical thinking.[2] Unlike mythos, logos corresponds to objective facts. Logos is wholly pragmatic: it is the rational mode of thought that enables human beings to function. It is the basis of our modern society. We use our logical powers when we want to make something happen, to achieve something or to persuade others to adopt a particular opinion. Where myth looks back to origins, logos forges ahead, develops new insights and invents something fresh. It also, for good and ill, helps us to achieve greater control over the natural environment.

But logos, like mythos, has limitations. It cannot answer questions about the ultimate value of human life. It cannot assuage our sorrow. It can unveil wonderful new facts about the physical universe and make things work more efficiently, but it cannot explain the meaning of life. From a very early period, *Homo sapiens* understood this instinctively. He used logos to develop new weapons and hunting skills; and he turned to myth, with its accompanying rituals, to reconcile him to the inevitable pain and grief that might otherwise overwhelm him.

Before the modern period, both mythos and logos were regarded as essential, but by the eighteenth century the people of Europe and America had achieved such astonishing success in science and technology that they began to discount myth as false and primitive. Society was no longer wholly dependent on a surplus of agricultural produce – like all previous civilisations – but relied increasingly on technological resources and the constant reinvestment of capital. This freed modern society from many of the constraints of traditional culture, whose agrarian base had always been precarious. The long process of modernisation took some three centuries and involved profound changes: industrialisation, the British agricultural revolution, the political reform of society and an intellectual 'enlightenment' that dismissed myth as futile and outmoded. Yet while our demythologised world may be comfortable for those of us fortunate enough to live in First World countries, it has not become the earthly paradise predicted by Francis Bacon and other Enlightenment philosophers.

We must disabuse ourselves of the fallacy that myth is untrue or represents an inferior mode of thought. We may be unable to return wholesale to a premodern sensibility, but we can acquire a more nuanced understanding of the myths of our ancestors because they still have something to teach us. And of course, we continue to create our own myths, even if we don't describe them as such. The twentieth century saw the emergence of some very destructive myths that ended in massacre and genocide. We cannot counter these bad myths with reason alone because undiluted logos cannot deal with deep-rooted fears, desires and neuroses. We need good myths that help us to identify with our fellow human beings, and not just with those who belong to our ethnic, national or ideological tribe. We need good myths that help us to realise the importance of compassion, which challenges and transcends our solipsistic and tribal egocentricity. And, crucially, we need good myths that help us to venerate the earth as sacred once again, because unless there is a spiritual revolution that challenges the destructiveness of our technological genius, we will not save our planet.

The great myths of the past presented the natural world as imbued with sacrality. But – I repeat – a myth makes no sense unless it is translated into practical action. Myths were not just cautionary tales: they had to be put into practice and were therefore always accompanied by ritual. Ritual, like myth, is often misunderstood in our pragmatic world; in the early modern period, it was rejected even by religious people as outdated superstition. Yet ritual ceremonies were indispensable to premodern religion, and they never were wholly spiritual affairs but involved the body and, through the body, the emotions. Neurophysicists tell us that, without being consciously aware of it, we receive and transmit important information through our senses, physical movements and gestures.[3] Carefully crafted rituals making use of emotive music, dance and drama can dramatically bring a mythical event of the distant past into the present. If devised with sufficient skill, they can also yield an aesthetic ecstasy that enables participants to 'stand outside' their mundane selves for a moment. By acting out a ritual role with skill and concentration, we can leave the self behind and, paradoxically, achieve self-enhancement. Through the arts we experience a more intense form of being and feel part of something larger, more momentous and complete.[4] Only if myth is translated into action do we discover its relevance and meaning.

Many of our ancestors' myths that we shall consider in this book taught them how to revere the natural environment. Unlike in our modern environmental discourse, nature was presented and experienced imaginatively and aesthetically rather than scientifically, and this involved the emotions and the body. In the next chapter, we shall see that different cultures across the world saw nature as imbued with the sacred in remarkably similar ways. Perhaps this perspective is built into the structure of the human mind. But the religious ceremonies were not just aesthetic exercises: they demanded practical commitment and response. We shall see that these rituals were hard work. They were time-consuming and demanding; they involved, quite literally, sacrifice. They not only expressed a deep anxiety about the sustainability of our world but made great demands on participants, who were expected not just to honour the divine in nature but also to reform themselves – to transcend their egos and reach out to all their fellow human beings. If today we have come to realise that devotion to the planet requires devotion to everything and everybody on it, then this is a perception that dates back to the very beginning of humanity.

The Way Forward

Our first task is to appreciate the value of myth and understand how myths work. This will require a re-evaluation of many of our presuppositions. We have to stop thinking of a myth as a charming story and instead discover its deeper meaning and what it requires us to do, both intellectually and practically. In the next chapter we shall look at concepts of nature that are strange to us and do not accord with our modern logos. Yet rather than dismissing them as simply fictional or mistaken, we should try to discover what kind of truth they were aiming to convey. Why did these ideas take such firm root in the minds and hearts of people across the world? Even if these myths bear little relation to scientific theory, they may express truth that has perennial value and should, therefore, find a place in our own thinking today.

Myth is not an inferior method of inquiry that can be cast aside when people have attained the age of reason. It is not an early attempt at history; it doesn't claim to be objectively true. Rather, it helps us to glimpse new possibilities. In art, liberated from the constraints of logos, we conceive and combine new forms of expression that enrich our lives and tell us something important, giving us fresh insight into the disturbing puzzle of our world. Thus a myth is true because it is effective. The myths that we shall consider persisted for centuries, because they *worked* when people translated them into action. A myth is essentially a guide: it tells us what to do to live more richly and effectively. The ancient myths about nature were an attempt to describe the hidden reality of the natural world and to live effectively and safely within our environment.

Each of the following chapters explores ideas, attitudes or practices that were essential to the way people experienced nature in the past. Each chapter offers a building block that will help us to create or rediscover within ourselves a new attitude towards the natural world and so deepen our spiritual commitment to the environment. Recycling and political protests are not enough. At the end of each chapter, we shall ask ourselves how we can translate a particular ideal into our everyday lives – practically, creatively and effectively. Each myth asks something of us and we have to discover what is within our means to put it into practice. A myth will mean different things to, and make demands of, different people. We have to find out what each myth is asking of us personally.

2

Sacred Nature

In the seventeenth century, Jesuit missionaries brought the new European science to China. The Chinese literati were intrigued and more than happy to consider such ideas as the relative positions of the celestial bodies, the phases of Venus and the existence of the primum mobile – ideas that had, at first, caused considerable consternation in Europe. But they were bewildered by the idea of a god boxed into a tenth 'quiescent' heaven on the outskirts of the cosmos. Why should the deity whom the Jesuits called the 'Lord of Creation' be content to be confined to a tiny sector of the universe that he had supposedly created? The Confucian scholar Fang Yizhi (1611–71) concluded that the West was 'detailed in material investigation', but deficient in 'comprehending seminal forces (*qi*)'. By *qi* Fang was referring to the essence of being – a force that the Chinese regarded as 'unknowable', the 'recondite, and the uniting layers of mysteries'. The Jesuits, Fang concluded, did not understand the limitations of language when speaking of the ultimate: 'Frequently their meanings are encumbered by their words.'[1] When faced with the ultimate reality, he believed, humans must fall silent because it lies beyond the reach of verbal concepts.

Qi challenged – and still challenges – Western ideas. It is the basic 'stuff' or essence of the universe and is neither wholly spiritual nor wholly material; it therefore falls outside all our usual categories. It is ineffable; it is something that we cannot define or describe. Qi is not a god or a being of any kind; it is the energy that pervades all life, harmoniously linking the plant, animal, human and divine worlds and enabling them to fulfil their potential. Where the seventeenth-century Jesuits saw a gulf between the human and divine worlds, with God benignly surveying humanity from the tenth heaven, the Chinese saw continuity. Together, heaven, earth and humanity formed a continuum – a triad that was organic, holistic and dynamic. The Confucian scholar Tu

Weiming (b. 1940) has described this integral relationship as 'anthropocosmic': there is no division between human beings and the cosmos, because the two share the same reality.[2]

In China, therefore, we encounter a very different worldview from in the West. The cosmos is in constant flux, activated by a vital force of which all things are composed and by which all things are linked. As one poem composed in the fourth century BCE explained, qi is

> The vital essence of all things:
> It is this that brings them to life.
> It generates the five grains below
> And becomes the constellated stars above.
> When flowing amid the heavens and the earth
> We call it ghostly and numinous.
> When stored within the chests of human beings,
> We call them sages.[3]

The Confucian sage, the perfected human being, is integrated perfectly with the human, divine and natural spheres. Where in the modern West we tend to separate the sacred from the human, the religious from the secular, the Confucian regards himself not as a creature but as a co-creator of the universe. He will not cultivate a wholly 'spiritual' life, therefore, contemplating a god dwelling in heaven; on the contrary, he must be attentive to his fellow beings, responsive to the needs of society, and deeply attuned to the natural world and the cosmos, all of which form a continuum with humankind.

Chinese religious traditions may be unique in having no creation story. Certainly they have no creator god. *Yin* and *yang*, the two opposing elements within qi, interact creatively in a process of continuous transformation to produce and sustain the material elements of the universe – rocks, mountains, rivers, plants, animals, humans. In China, therefore, human beings were neither privileged nor unique but, together with the *wanwu*, the 'myriad' or 'ten thousand things' of nature, formed 'one body with the universe'. This idea is still so widely accepted in both popular and higher culture that it can be said to be a genuinely Chinese worldview.

Consequently, the Chinese philosopher Mencius (*c.* 372–289 BCE) insisted that the Golden Rule first promulgated by Confucius in the sixth century BCE – 'Do not impose on others what you yourself do not desire'[4] – applies not only to our fellow humans but also to the wanwu, to which we are inextricably connected.

> All the ten thousand things are there in me. There is no greater joy for me to find, on self-examination, that I am true to myself. Try your best to treat others as you would wish to be treated yourself, and you will find that this is the shortest way to humanity (*ren*).[5]

We see beauty in the wanwu and when we try to describe a tree, mountain or river, we move from its physical appearance to the spiritual vitality at its core, and finally to qi, which pervades all things. So we must treat all the wanwu, the 'things' of nature, as we would wish to be treated ourselves, because we share the same vital force.

Mencius was a sophisticated philosopher, but Laozi, the fourth-century BCE founder of Daoism, described himself as an outsider who was dismissed as clumsy, gloomy and uncouth by the supposedly 'clever' people. But, he claimed, he had had an ecstatic experience of the Absolute, the hidden root of the whole of existence. Unlike Confucianism, which originated within the aristocratic gentry, Daoism was rooted in the indigenous, tribal culture of southern China, a region of wild marshes, rivers, forests and mountains, whose peoples did not participate in Chinese civilisation. Laozi himself, however, was born in the nearby state of Song, home of the descendants of the Shang dynasty, which had ruled China until 1045 BCE and were settled there after its defeat. They had preserved their ancient shamanistic culture. In the *Shenhaijing* ('Classic of Mountains and Seas'), a source book of ancient Chinese mythology, there is a description of a divine bird that was revered by tribal people but bore no relation to reality as we know it: it had six legs, four wings and no eyes or face, but it was expert at the singing and dancing that traditionally accompanied shamanistic worship. Laozi and his near contemporary, the Daoist philosopher Zhuangzi (369–286 BCE), were moved by these tribal spiritualities, but as sophisticated members of Chinese society they could no longer fully share the shaman's vision.

Laozi revived the ancient notion of the Dao, the sacred principle of nature that may have been revered by the Song and other early Chinese people. But, the product of an increasingly sophisticated urban civilisation, Laozi developed this concept philosophically. In the enigmatic verses of the *Daodejing* ('Classic of the Way and its Power') the Dao becomes the ineffable, unknowable source of being manifest in the *de*, the sacred 'power' that makes every 'thing' that exists what it is and ought to be.

With an intuitive, contemplative state of mind, Laozi had glimpsed a dynamic, sacred force at the heart of mundane existence – a vision he described in the deliberately enigmatic verses of the *Daodejing*. When it appeared in China in the fourth century BCE, it had an immediate impact, as though the readers recognised and were eager to rediscover an ancient, precious insight.

> The way (*dao*) that can be spoken of
>   is not the constant way;
> The name that can be named
>   is not the constant name.
> The nameless was the beginning of heaven and
>   earth.
> The named was the mother of the myriad
>   creatures (*wanwu*).[6]

Dao, like qi, lies beyond the reach of words. Yet if we manage to enter the deeper regions of our mind we can embark on a mystical descent to the ineffable heart of being, the 'Mystery upon Mystery'. Laozi suggests that we should call it 'the Dark' and 'the gateway of the manifold secrets', because it conceals more than it reveals.[7] So instead of defining the Dao, Laozi described it as a process – the 'way' we have to take to discover true reality. Perpetually hidden and endlessly elusive, the Dao lies beyond thought and logic: in purely rational terms, it is simply 'no-thing'. But if we carefully change our mode of perception, we see that it is pregnant with reality.

The Dao, Laozi explains, reaches outwards, endlessly emanating from the sublime unknown until, stage by stage, it brings our world into existence.[8] Crucially, if paradoxically, Laozi described this process as a 'return'.

> Turning back is how the way moves;
> Weakness is the means it employs.
> The myriad creatures in the world are born from Something, and Something from Nothing (*wu*).[9]

All things have their origin in this sacred source, and, Laozi explains, they constantly return to it. Thus nothing that we know or see is stable. Everything that seems firm and secure is in motion, circling perpetually from the ineffable source to our world and back again. The only permanent force is the Dao itself.

Laozi calls the Dao the 'granary of the ten-thousand things' – of wanwu.[10] It is, as it were, a place where all things wait *in potentia* until they become physically manifest in our world in a three-stage process:

> The Dao begets one; one begets two, two begets three, three begets the myriad creatures.[11]

The Dao is not the 'creator' of the ten thousand things, looking down on them benignly from afar. Rather, Laozi explains, it is their 'mother' and the two are inseparable. Indeed, we cannot know one without the other:

> The world has a source: the world's mother.
> Once you have the mother,
>   You know the children.
> Once you know the children,
>   Return to the mother.[12]

Heaven-and-earth – the cosmos comprising our material world – and the ten thousand things are simply stages in the Dao's own evolution. It is the extraordinary force that holds everything together, makes the world productive and keeps it in being. Every single thing that exists is what it is because it is animated by the creative activity of the Dao.

But the Dao is not an invasive, alien, controlling power. Rather, everything *is* the Dao. It is, therefore, the *de* ('nature') of each creature; it is its identity, the force that makes it what it truly is. Thus every single 'thing' in the world – animal, plant or mineral – embodies the One in its own unique way. What's more, these 'things' are not self-centred; each manifests itself in an environment where it interacts harmoniously with the de of all the other things in its vicinity – in rather the same way that each ingredient in a stew blends with and enhances the others.

Unlike the all-powerful creator of the Hebrew Bible, who commands the world into being, the Dao is weak, according to Laozi. Creation is not an act of power and domination; the Dao is formless and flows through all things, offering itself to each creature and allowing it to thrive. 'Being weak is how the Dao works',[13] Laozi tells us. Once settled on earth, the 'myriad things' flourish for a while, but eventually begin their 'return' to the rich darkness of the One – a process that Laozi, who has managed to cultivate the visionary powers of the shaman, has been able to observe.

The myriad creatures all rise together
And I watch their return.

The teeming creatures
All return to their separate roots.
Returning to one's roots is known as stillness.[14]

The *jing* ('stillness') that the myriad things enjoy is, therefore, a return to their original source. It can be compared with the seasonal cycle of a plant that grows exuberantly in the spring, forming flowers or fruit, but in winter sends its energy down into its roots. Jing, therefore, is not the stillness of death; it is a stillness infused with the vitality of the Dao which will spring to life again. So the creative energy of the Dao is cyclical, revealing itself in a perpetual return.

While each 'thing' reflects the Dao's activity in a unique way, ironically, the human being – who should be the most perfect embodiment of the Dao – is the only creature with the mental ability to obstruct or distort their sacred identity with egotism. So how do we achieve insight into the way things really are? Zhuangzi suggests that we observe the Dao in nature. While Laozi presents the Dao as a circular process we can discover in ourselves, Zhuangzi was less interested in describing the Dao, which is, after all, ineffable. He wanted to show his readers how they could achieve this mystical insight. They had to let their 'selves' go. Once we stop trying – pointlessly – to preserve and promote our fragile, moribund identity, we begin to realise that all beings – ourselves included – are just transitory instances of the Dao's endless self-manifestation. Because the Dao's constant coming and going is especially evident in nature, Zhuangzi urges us to focus our attention on the natural world with such intensity that we 'forget' ourselves and thereby experience transcendence.

Zhuangzi frequently introduces us to ordinary individuals engaged in seemingly humdrum tasks who have achieved *ekstasis* – a loss of self – by immersing themselves in the natural world. Zhuangzi had little time for Confucianism but, often mischievously, he uses Confucius as his spokesman. One day, he tells us, Confucius was travelling through a forest and saw a hunchback catching cicadas with astonishing ease. 'Is there a special way to do this?' he asked. The hunchback replied:

> I hold my body stiff like a dry tree trunk and use my arm like an old dry limb. No matter how huge heaven and earth or how numerous the ten thousand things, I'm aware of nothing but cicada wings. No wavering, no tipping, not letting any other of the other ten thousand things take the place of cicada wings – how can I help but succeed?[15]

The hunchback had left his mundane self behind; by focusing so intensely on the 'things' of nature, he had in some way sensed qi. He was not seeking a supernatural God in the distant heavens; he was aligning himself with the mysterious, ineffable force that governs the natural world. By forgetting her 'self', the Daoist becomes one with the way things truly are, realising that the apparent contradictions of life form a numinous unity. This is not a rapturous, ecstatic experience; nor is it always a solitary quest. When, Zhuangzi tells us, Daoists discussed the insoluble mysteries of life together, filled with quiet awe, they simply 'looked at one another and smiled. There was no disagreement in their hearts, and so [they] became friends.'[16] Because the Dao is present within us, there is no need for learned discourse – we simply have to abandon ego and align ourselves with sacred nature. Instead of clinging to his opinions and becoming quarrelsome, the sage develops what we might call a right-hemispheric view of the world in which opposites unite, enabling him to have a transcendent vision of the Dao.

The Dao and qi are both very different from our Western God; they are closer to what Thomas Aquinas called 'Being itself', and this seems to have been how most humans once perceived the divine. This was certainly the case in India. The Aryan pastoralists who arrived in the Punjab in about 1500 BCE had a segmented society, consisting of three classes: the *Brahmin* priests and the warrior *Kshatriyas*, which comprised the aristocracy, and the *Vaishyas* or 'commoners' which served them. Engaged in remorseless conflict and constantly imperilled by drought and famine, the Indo-Aryans nevertheless experienced the natural world as a place of beauty and wonder, inhabited by hidden divine forces which they called the 'shining ones' or 'devas'.

This vision had been revealed to them not by rational thinkers but by their poets – the *rishis* or 'seers'. The beauty of their verse, sung to a ritual chant, shocked their audiences into a state of such wonder and delight that they too felt touched by a divine power.[17] The rishis seem to have achieved a mental alertness that would later inform the techniques of yoga. They discovered that it was possible to contemplate the world so intensively that nature seemed imbued with divinity. They lived, they believed, in a three-tiered universe consisting of 'Earth', 'Sky' and 'Heaven', which was inhabited by the devas. In the stars, the rishis saw the luminous eyes of the goddess Ratri or 'Night';[18] the rivers revealed the sparkling, chattering, ever-flowing

Sarasvati, who brought them life and prosperity; the lightning was Indra's thunderbolt; the wind was Vata 'who breaks things into pieces as it passes by, making a sound like thunder';[19] while Usas, the dawn, unmasked her beauty every morning, like a wife revealing herself to her husband.[20]

The rishis attributed their poetic power to the hallucinogenic plant *soma*, which enabled them to look beneath the surface of things and discover a deva in every single one, so nature was alive, imbued with the divine. They called the faculty they had cultivated *dhi* ('insight'); it gave them a knowledge (*veda*) that bore no relation to mundane awareness. Their poems suggest that they had momentary glimpses of the devas that came to them in a series of 'stills' – static, unconnected images, with no clear theological message.[21] They also heard *Vac*, the sacred 'Word' that had shaped the cosmic order and still dwelt deeply within it.

All these divine forces, the rishis concluded, were grounded in a mysterious omnipresent power, which they called *Rta*, one of the most important concepts in the *Vedas*, the ancient texts of Hinduism. Rta is best understood as 'active, creative truth' or 'the way things truly are'.[22] Like qi and the Dao, Rta was not a god but a sacred, impersonal, animating force. It was impossible to describe or define Rta, but it could be experienced as the sublime whole, which flowed from itself expansively, bringing about the cosmos, humans and the gods themselves. The fact that for most of history people in different parts of the world developed such a remarkably similar conception of this sacred reality suggests that it may be an archetypal notion embedded in the human psyche.[23]

The rishis expressed their vision of the universe in mythos rather than scientific logos. In their poems, they explained that after the devas had emerged from the primal force of Rta, they created the three-tiered cosmos and made it viable. Mitra and Varuna, for example, calculated the dimensions of space, placed the rising sun in the heavens, and produced water to make the soil fertile. Rta can be translated as 'the artfulness of being' and is the Indic root of the English words 'harmony' and 'art'. As products of Rta, the devas were artists and achieved the immense task of creation through their imagination. First, they pictured these non-existent realities in their minds. Then, in a quite extraordinary feat, they managed to project these mental images into the physical world they were furnishing. The rishis called this miraculous process *maya*. The force of the devas' minds had enabled them to translate their mental ideas into material objects – clouds, grass, mountains and trees – and position them aesthetically in our physical world.[24]

But after creating and organising the world, the devas did not return to heaven. They took up residence in the natural phenomena they had brought into being and dwelt forever within them.[25] Thus every single bird, animal or flower embodied the divinity that had created it, and everything in the world had a sacred core. Instead of merely shining on things from afar, the devas remained embedded in the mundane, 'entering into this world through their hidden nature'.[26] In the modern West, we have carefully developed an analytical worldview, which separates the material from the psychological and the spiritual, but the Aryans had a more holistic vision and were aesthetically aware of the presence of *Rta* in nature. The divine was not confined to the 'distant deeps and skies' of heaven, therefore; it permeated the whole of reality. Nothing was purely material but everything – including human beings – was imbued with sacred potency and fitted together 'artistically'.[27]

By about the sixth century BCE, however, the Aryans were redefining the ultimate reality; and they called it the Brahman. While Rta had been the eternal *principle* of being that informed and permeated the universe, the Brahman was the *foundation* of all reality, the 'beingness' on which all things depended. This development was part of a new spirituality called *Vedanta* ('the end of the Vedas'), which sought to reveal the essential purpose of the ancient rites. Whereas the early rishis had depicted the gods poetically as different aspects of the one divine reality, the Vedantic priests now expressed this insight philosophically. The Brahman was the one and only sacred *Atman* ('Self') of the entire universe.[28] It pervaded everything and every person 'right up to the tips of the fingernails'.[29] It 'lives in each and every being. Uniform, yet multiform, it appears like the [reflection of the single] moon in [the many ripples of] a pond'.[30] The people of India would never lose this insight. While we in the modern West have confined God to the heavens, they have continued to emphasise the ubiquity of the sacred throughout the world, even when they later came to personify the supreme reality, calling it Shiva, Vishnu or the 'Divine Mother'.[31]

In addition, the Vedantic priests now sought to experience the Brahman within themselves as well as in nature.[32] They were beginning to realise that the ultimate reality – be it Rta or the Brahman – not only pervaded the natural world but also was the sacred core of their own selves, and they taught their students to become aware of this. Each human being is a unique expression of the Atman. The sage Sanatkumara insisted that knowledge of the Vedas required a mastery of not only the texts but the intricacies of ritual, and ethical debate. Also essential was 'the science of government, the science of the heavenly bodies, and the science of serpent beings; and the sky, earth, wind, space, water, fire, gods, humans, domestic animals, birds, grasses, trees, and wild beasts, down to the very worms, moths, and ants'.[33] These beings were not inert; rather, they were all infused by the Brahman and, like humans, they mirrored the ultimate reality at the core of their being and thus ceaselessly returned to it. 'The earth in a sense is reflecting deeply; the intermediate region in a sense is reflecting deeply; the sky in a sense is reflecting deeply; the waters in a sense are reflecting deeply; the hills in a sense are reflecting deeply; and gods and men are reflecting deeply.'[34]

India reminds us that the sense of the sacred is best learned aesthetically – in poetry, music and ritual. It is pointless to try to prove these ancient insights rationally, because they require imagination and the ability to see what is not apparent, as Jean-Paul Sartre explained.[35] The ultimate reality – be it Brahman, Rta, the Dao, or indeed 'God' – does not exist like anything in our ordinary experience. It can be intuited only with the allusive and emotive arts.

So deeply was humanity's religious impulse connected with the sacrality of nature that even a religious tradition such as Buddhism – which originally focused on the method of introspection by which humans could be liberated from sorrow – eventually turned to nature. When Mahayana Buddhism arrived in China, it insisted that the Buddhata – the 'Buddha-Nature' or the potential to achieve Buddhahood and Enlightenment – was not confined to human beings but inherent in plants, rocks, trees and blades of grass. In the *Dacheng qixin lun* ('Awakening of Faith'), a sixth-century CE text, we learn that the Buddha-Nature is the essence of the entire cosmos, an 'eternal, permanent, immutable, pure, and self-sufficient force that unites all beings, draws them into a coherent whole, and universally illumines the mind of man and enables him to cultivate his capacity for goodness (*ren*)'.[36] Not only do all things have the capacity for enlightenment, but existence itself is an expression of the Buddha-Nature.

The Daoists had developed a form of contemplation called 'quiet sitting', which emptied the mind of preconceived ideas and made it more receptive to outside influences. Chinese Buddhists developed this practice to make themselves aware of the intense activity of sacred nature, which was also striving for Nirvana. Opening his mind to the sights and sounds of nature, the Buddhist recluse 'sits quietly' and forgets himself. Losing his normal preoccupation with the self, he stays in the present, like the things of nature 'at peace from dust and delusion . . . still as the waters of the autumn river'.[37] He tries to return his mind to its original stillness, so that, mirror-like, it will perfectly reflect the potential for enlightenment that is inherent in all things.

In Japan, Zen Buddhists believe that a single Buddha-Nature exists in the things of nature and that it is inseparable from the human self. The aim of Zen is to cultivate awareness of its existence, making it a reality within oneself. Zen spirituality enables us to perceive the Buddha-Nature in both the natural world and in human beings in ways that depend not on authoritative texts but on the right hemisphere of the brain.[38] 'The world now appears as if dressed in a new garment, which seems to cover up the unsightliness of dualism,' the Japanese scholar D. T. Suzuki (1870–1966) explained:

> There is something rejuvenating in the possession of Zen. The spring flowers look prettier, and the mountain stream runs cooler and more

> transparent. The subjective revolution that brings about this state of things cannot be called abnormal. When life becomes more enjoyable and its expanse broadens to include the universe itself, there must be something in satori [the potential for enlightenment] that is quite precious and well worth striving after.[39]

We get a glimpse of the Zen perception of nature in the writings of the thirteenth-century philosopher-poet Zenji Dōgen Kigen (1200–53), who established a particularly austere version of Zen in the Japanese mountains after studying Buddhism in China for several years. For Dōgen, all being is the Buddha-Nature. He did not mean that the Buddha-Nature was somehow 'hidden' in plants, trees and flowers; it was not a seed or germ of sacrality concealed within the physical world that would one day flower. For Dōgen, the phenomenal world simply and literally *was* the Buddha-Nature, since all things have the same sacred potential and are all, in their own ways, striving for Nirvana – and achieving it.

This strong sense of inherent sacrality recurs in nearly every religious tradition. It seems to be more instinctive to the human mind than our modern habit of devitalising the natural world and transforming it into matter that can be manipulated for human purposes. We even find it in monotheism, which had initially presented God as transcending the natural world. It seems that the medieval Jewish mystics who pioneered the tradition of the Kabbalah were, in part, responding to a popular demand for a more immanent notion of the sacred. For the Kabbalists, the deeds of God recorded in the Bible were simply symbols of a mysterious divine process, so they turned on its head the historical claim that God had created the world 'out of nothing', and suggested that creation had proceeded stage by stage 'out of God'. 'Nothing', therefore, was not a blank emptiness: it was God; it was being itself and thus more real than any other proposed entity. It was 'nothing' only in human terms because the innermost core of divinity remains forever unknowable, bearing no relationship with anything in our human experience. Kabbalists called this hidden core of the divine *En Sof* ('without end'). But the remote and unknowable En Sof contains within the deepest recesses of its being aspects of divinity that are also present in creation. So there is a deeply hidden primary world that is wholly immaterial and unintelligible, but also a secondary world adjoining it that is physical, which makes it possible for all creatures to gain some knowledge of the sacred.

This Kabbalistic cosmology posits ten *sephiroth* ('spheres' or 'worlds of light'), all pulsing with divine life, that form a sort of bridge between the unknowable En Sof and our material world. These are not cosmic 'stages' between our world and God; nor are they like the steps of a ladder between us and an exalted divinity. Rather, each sephirah represents a phase in the gradual manifestation of the Unknowable, each one revealing a little more about the utterly mysterious God that emerges stage by stage from its profound concealment and, as it were, descends step by step from the innermost recesses of divinity until it reaches the world.

We find a similar notion in the theology of a Byzantine monk who called himself Denys the Areopagite after St Paul's first Athenian convert[40] and taught in Alexandria in the late fifth and early sixth centuries.[41] Like the Kabbalists, Denys regarded creation as a kind of intimate outpouring of divine goodness into all things – an ekstasis in which the One 'stands outside' itself to participate in the existence of creation while still retaining its mysterious 'apartness':

> The very Cause of the universe . . . is, as it were, beguiled by goodness, by love, and by

> yearning and is enticed away from his transcendent dwelling place and comes to abide within all things, and he does so by virtue of his supernatural and ecstatic capacity to remain, nevertheless, within himself.[42]

But instead of the mysterious and elusive emanations of the Kabbalah, Denys unashamedly depicts the creative ecstasy as orgasmic. For this Christian monk, it is more like a volcanic eruption. But while lava hardens and cools the further it flows, each being, however lowly, remains indelibly transformed by God: each has the same immediate relationship with the divine. So, unlike the Kabbalah, where each emanation is progressively more distant from En Sof, every single creature – be it an earthworm or an archangel – enjoys an equal relationship with the sacred.

Denys experienced nature as pointing beyond itself to the ineffability that we call God. We can only intuit God's presence through the veils of natural objects, which conceal as much as they reveal. If we could see God clearly, it would not be God. But if we learn to contemplate nature correctly, we find that the tiniest particle of soil can yield a glimpse of the ineffable divine.

The Way Forward

How can we recover this vision of a sacred nature?

First, I think, by altering our perception of 'God'. Instead of seeing 'Him' confined to the distant heavens, we need to look to this older – and still widespread – understanding of the divine as an inexpressible but dynamic inner presence that flows through all things. This notion seems to have come more naturally to people than the image of a solitary creator, and it was how Western people regarded the divine until the late Middle Ages.

In his poem 'Tintern Abbey' William Wordsworth tells us that he taught himself to look at nature differently. As a young man, he had responded instinctively and emotionally to the natural world, but now he finds that to plumb its depths, nature requires more intensive contemplation. He can no longer just luxuriate in nature for its own sake, because he has discovered that it is inseparable from:

> The still sad music of humanity
> Nor harsh, nor grating, though of
> ample power
> To chasten and subdue.[43]

Today that link between nature and humanity has become even more poignant, as we consider the damage we have inflicted on our environment. We cannot delight in nature any more without knowing that we face the urgent task of saving it from human destruction.

But then Wordsworth goes on to describe the sacred presence that he experiences in the natural world. Importantly he will not call it 'God'. Wordsworth nearly always chooses his words extremely carefully. In conversation, we often use the word 'something' vaguely to refer to an event or a feeling that is indistinct or obscure. But Wordsworth uses it judiciously for a reality that he will not – indeed, cannot – define.

> And I have felt
> A presence that disturbs me with the joy
> Of elevated thoughts; a sense sublime
> Of something far more deeply interfused,
> Whose dwelling is the light of setting suns,
> And the round ocean, and the living air,
> And the blue sky, and in the mind of man.
> A motion and a spirit that impels
> All thinking things, all objects of all thought,
> And rolls through all things.[44]

Does this not remind us more forcibly of Rta and Brahman, qi and the Dao, than the modern Western God?

If we allow it to enter our lives, nature can inform our minds and become a formative influence. We can begin by taking simple steps, perhaps sitting in a garden or a park for ten minutes a day, without headphones or a mobile phone, simply registering the sights and sounds of nature. Instead of taking photographs of our surroundings, we should look at the birds, flowers, clouds and trees and let them impress themselves on our minds. In another of his poems, Wordsworth speaks of the 'wise passiveness' that should inform our dealings with nature. He is arguing with somebody who has his nose in a book all the time, blocking out all the sights and sounds of the natural world – it is hard to imagine what he would have thought of our technology today! We don't need learned books, Wordsworth tells us, because our senses drink in the secrets of nature without our being aware of it.

> The eye – it cannot choose but see;
> We cannot bid the ear be still;
> Our bodies feel, where'er they be,
> Against or with our will.

Nor less I deem that there are Powers
Which of themselves our minds impress;
That we can feed this mind of ours
In a wise passiveness.[45]

In the same way, we can train ourselves in what the Chinese called 'quiet sitting' and learn to note the common life that flows through all things, linking them together in harmonious unity. As we sit and watch our natural environment, we should make ourselves aware of the way that birds and leaves, the clouds and the wind, harmonise so that we are not watching a score of different objects but a whole in which each thing has its perfect place. If we develop a mind that 'watches and receives'[46] and discover the fluidity of our natural environment, we may be able to recover some of our ancestors' vision of a sacred nature.

3

The Holiness of Nature

These days we tend to use the words 'holy' and 'holiness' rather lightly to describe something or someone who is spiritually perfect, morally excellent and dedicated to God. But the Hebrew word *qaddosh*, which we translate as 'holiness', means 'otherness', implying a radical separation from everyday reality. When Yahweh, the God of Israel, appeared to Moses on Mount Sinai, the nimbus of glory that surrounded him seemed like a devouring fire.[1] When the Prophet Isaiah had a vision of Yahweh in the temple, the seraphs who cried 'holy, holy, holy!' were proclaiming that God was 'other, other, other!'[2] Isaiah had experienced that sense of the numinous that periodically descends upon men and women. The philosopher of religion Rudolf Otto (1869–1937) described this fearful experience of transcendent reality as the *mysterium tremendum et fascinans*: '*tremendum*' because it comes as a profound shock that tears us away from the consolations of everyday life; and '*fascinans*' because, at the same time, it exerts an irresistible attraction. The emotions it arouses cannot adequately be expressed in words or concepts. Indeed, this overpowering experience of the wholly other cannot even be said to 'exist' because it has no place in our normal scheme of reality.[3]

So in what sense can nature be 'holy'? Because of the damage we have done to our environment, we tend to see nature as delicate and vulnerable. But this is a simplistic view: as we know too well, nature can be fierce. Tornadoes, volcanic eruptions, floods, earthquakes and wildfires remind us that it has deadly power. As I write, the whole world has been paralysed by a virus that, despite our scientific brilliance, we are finding difficult to control. The coronavirus pandemic has taken millions of lives, shaken economies and deprived us of many of the freedoms on which we pride ourselves in the Western world. So nature, like the divine, can be *tremendum* as well as *fascinans*. It can easily segue from the role of victim to that of destroyer.

Israel, as we have seen, experienced the divine in history rather than the natural world. So instead of finding the sacred in the phenomena of nature, the Hebrew scriptures focus on the victories and disasters, battles and plagues, that befell the Israelites: their god Yahweh was not immanent in the wondrously repetitive rhythms of nature; he revealed himself in the convulsions of history. This break with most other religious traditions became clear in about 1250 BCE, when Moses, who was tending a flock of sheep, saw something strange – a bush that was on fire but not burnt up. When he stepped closer to investigate, Yahweh called to him from the bush. Other Middle Eastern religions would have regarded this divinity as inseparable from the burning shrub – as the numinous force that enabled it to exist, thrive and flourish. But Yahweh dissociated himself from the bush – from nature – and allied himself with Moses' ancestors. He was the God of Abraham, Isaac and Jacob, who made himself known in the events of history.[4]

But this radical break with tradition was not achieved overnight. In the ninth century BCE, the prophet Elijah was engaged in a conflict with the followers of the fertility god Baal in northern Canaan. At this time, most Israelites still found the idea of worshipping a single god bizarre. Yahweh was a god of war who had helped them conquer the promised land. He had little known expertise in agriculture, whereas Baal made their fields fertile, enhanced their understanding of the natural world and gave meaning to their back-breaking struggle against sterility and famine. In the cult of Baal, they felt that they encountered the sacred energies that made the earth productive.[5] After a deadly skirmish with Baal's priests, Elijah had to flee the wrath of the people and took refuge on Mount Horeb to await Yahweh's arrival.

> There came a mighty wind, so strong it tore the mountains and shattered the rocks before Yahweh. But Yahweh was not in the wind. After the wind came an earthquake. But Yahweh was not in the earthquake. After the earthquake came a fire. But Yahweh was not in the fire. And after the fire there came the sound of a gentle breeze. And when Elijah heard this, he covered his face with a cloak.[6]

Unlike his fellow Israelites who worshipped Baal, Elijah no longer experienced the sacred in the convulsions and rhythms of nature. For him, Yahweh had become so distant from the natural world that he was scarcely perceptible – expressed only in the timbre of a light breeze.

Throughout the Hebrew scriptures, the sacred is usually celebrated not as an immanent presence but as a distant reality. Unlike the Indian devas, the God of Israel has not hidden himself in the natural world; nor is the sacred present in everyday reality, as in the wanwu of Daoism. Instead Yahweh is presented as the creator and ruler of the cosmos. When the psalmist looks up at the moon and the stars that his God single-handedly set in place, he does not dwell on their extraordinary beauty and inherent sanctity. His thoughts almost immediately turn to man, whom Yahweh has appointed the ruler of nature:

> You have made him little less than a god,
> you have crowned him in glory and splendour,
> made him lord over the work of your hands,
> set all things under his feet.

Everything in the universe, the psalmist exults, is subservient to humanity – sheep, oxen, wild animals, the 'birds of the air and the fish in the sea'.[7] In another psalm, the marvels of nature have been reduced to mere accessories of the divine:

> You stretch out the heavens like a tent,
> you build your palace on the waters above;

using the clouds as your chariot,
you advance on the wings of the wind;
you use the winds as messengers
and fiery flames as servants.[8]

No longer divine themselves, the natural elements are totally reliant on Yahweh:

You turn your face away, they suffer,
you stop their breath, they die
and revert to dust.
You give them breath, fresh life begins
you keep renewing the world.[9]

In the Book of Job, however, we find a very different approach to nature, which is expressed in some of the most passionate and beautiful poetry in the Bible.[10] Based on an ancient folk tale, this dramatic poem seems to have been composed by an Israelite who was involved in the Wisdom movement, which emerged in various religious traditions around the world and saw nature rather than the gods as the true source of morality. In Israel, the Wisdom teachers revered King Solomon as the quintessential sage:

> He could talk about plants from the cedars in Lebanon to the hyssop growing on the wall; and he could talk about animals, and birds and reptiles and fish. Men from all nations came to hear Solomon's wisdom, and he received gifts from all the kings of the world, who had heard of his wisdom.[11]

During the seventh century, editors known as the Deuteronomists composed a second (Greek: *deutero-*) history of Israel in the biblical books of Deuteronomy and Kings. They emphasised the importance of God's revelation to Moses on Mount Sinai and were challenged by the Wisdom writers, who argued that the lessons we learned from the natural world were just as important as the Ten Commandments. But the author of the Book of Job went further, arguing that nature shattered the narrow ethics of Sinai.

He tells us that Satan persuaded God to put Job, a famously righteous man, to the test and God obliged by inflicting a series of disasters on him and his household. His extensive livestock – oxen, sheep and camels – was destroyed; a thunderbolt fell on his house, killing all his children; and Job himself was struck with a hideous disease, which covered him with malignant ulcers from head to foot. His three friends, loyal advocates of the Wisdom movement, tried to comfort Job but also argued that God could not have treated him so cruelly if he were not guilty of serious sin. But Job stubbornly insisted on his innocence, loudly lamenting his fate. Falling into profound despair, he cursed the day he was born:

> May that day be darkness,
> may God on high have no thought for it,
> may no light shine on it,
> May murk and deep shadow claim it for
> their own.[12]

Entrenched in his all-too-human egotism, he turns his back on the entire cosmos. Why, he demands to know, should a virtuous man suffer? It is a typically anthropocentric question and when God finally responds to Job, he pointedly ignores it.

Instead, God compels Job to face up to the limitations of his understanding, bombarding him with questions of his own that Job finds impossible to answer.[13] God reveals a cosmic order of staggering beauty in which violence and suffering are essential to the life of all species and also, paradoxically, to their glory, because the animals rise so magnificently to these challenges. Instead of repining and lamenting the hardships they endure, they become even more courageous and splendid. Human beings would do well to follow their example. Instead of whining self-indulgently like Job, they must learn that they are not the centre of the world. Their parochial vision is not only blinkered but pusillanimous and wholly inappropriate. For the first and only time in the Bible, we see that nature has its own intrinsic value, power, integrity and beauty. Where Job had seen darkness and death, God reveals a cosmos pulsing with energy and life. Whereas Job had yearned for non-existence, God reveals the glory of the first dawn and the primal sea leaping triumphantly out of the womb of darkness, compelling him to confront the inadequacy of his vision:

> Where were you when I laid the earth's
>   foundations? . . .
> Who laid its cornerstone
> when all the stars of the morning were singing
>   with joy
>   and the Sons of God in chorus were
>   chanting praise?
> Who pent up the Sea behind closed doors
> when it leapt tumultuous out of the womb,

when I wrapped it in a robe of mist
  and made it fast with a bolted gate?[14]

Had Job any idea of how vast the earth is? Had he seen where the snow is kept? Could he fasten the harness of the Pleiades? Could he grasp the celestial laws and make the clouds and pent-up waters do his bidding?

Human beings may think they are the centre of the universe, God insists, but animals have far nobler values than the humans who exploit them. The mountain goats give birth to their calves and nurture them, but they don't hang on to their offspring as humans do; when they are grown, they 'leave them, never to return', allowing them perfect liberty. In the desert, where God intended him to live, the wild donkey is free, living proudly with no rope round his neck and never having to hear the cruel shouts of a driver. Humans think that the ostrich is stupid to lay her eggs on the ground where anyone can tread on them: 'Yet, if she bestirs herself to use her height, she can make fools of horse and rider too.'[15] And how could Job think that he rivals the beauty and magnificence of the horse?

Are you the one who makes the horse so brave
  and covers his neck with flowing hair?
Do you make him leap like a grasshopper?

His proud neighing spreads terror far and
wide.
Exultantly he paws the soil of the valley,
and prances eagerly to meet the clash of arms.
He laughs at fear; he is afraid of nothing,
he recoils before no sword.
On his back the quiver rattles,
the flashing spear and javelin,
Quivering with impatience, he eats up the miles;
when the trumpet sounds there is no holding
him.[16]

But it is Behemoth, the hippopotamus, whose immense strength – 'his bones as hard as hammered iron' – makes him 'the masterpiece of all God's work'. God has forbidden him to live in the mountain regions lest he endanger other animals, so he lies serenely beside the Nile, his massive strength voluntarily in abeyance:

The leaves of the lotus give him shade,
the willows by the stream shelter him.
Should the river overflow on him, why should
he worry?[17]

Behemoth symbolises the harmony of conflicting opposites in nature that epitomises the sacred. Thus nature shocks us out of our human complacency and forces us to confront the limitations of our vision. In nature we have a harmony in which violence and beauty, terror and serenity, mysteriously coexist, defying our own restricted categories.

When Yahweh reaches the end of his questions, he asks Job for his response. All Job can say is, 'My words have been frivolous, what can I reply?' Humbly, he puts his hand to his mouth, a ritual expression of awe in the presence of the sublime. He has experienced a revelation that recalls the theophany of Sinai when nature responded exuberantly to the divine presence with 'peals of thunder on the mountain and lightning flashes, a dense cloud, and a loud trumpet blast'.[18] Job, the author of the biblical poem seems to suggest, is a new Moses, a prophet to whom God has revealed the beauty, strength and mystery of sacred nature that pushes against the limited horizons of human beings.[19] Still, Job was a prophet unrecognised in Israel. Perhaps at this perilous juncture in our history it is time to acknowledge him.

The Way Forward

What is the Book of Job trying to tell us? There are no clear teachings or directions. God does not really answer any of Job's questions; instead, he dazzles him with an overwhelmingly eloquent description of nature that finally reduces even the loquacious Job to silence. This, the author implies, is the only possible response. Job, who throughout the poem has been bombastic and overconfident in his assertions of righteousness, and never at a loss for words, raises his hand to cover his mouth, realising that he is in the presence of something beyond the scope of his understanding. The extraordinary outpouring of words – the finest poetry in the Bible – engenders silence.

We have become averse to silence in the modern world and rely on endless chatter and stimulation. But in the presence of holiness, we should fall silent. As soon as we try to describe or define the sacred, we constrict and distort it. In the tenth century BCE, the Brahmin priests of India developed a contest called the *Brahmodya* that could be a model for us all. The goal was to find a verbal formula to define the Brahman by pushing language as far as it could go until it broke down, making the participants vividly aware of the ineffable. The challenger would ask a puzzling question and his opponent's reply had to be apt but equally inscrutable. The winner was the contestant who reduced his opponents to silence, for in that silence the Brahman was present, manifest in the stunning realisation of the impotence of speech.[20]

We have seen that the Dao is equally beyond our grasp. 'The Dao that can be named is not the eternal Dao,' Laozi tells us. You cannot say anything about it because it transcends our categories; all the distinctions that characterise our normal modes of thought become irrelevant. Christian monks who sought solitude in the Egyptian desert from the third century CE also cultivated a wordless spirituality that brought them *hesychia* ('tranquillity'). For them prayer was not a conversation with God or a structured meditation on divine nature. It meant a 'shedding of thoughts'. Because God lay beyond all thoughts and concepts, there could be no exalted feelings, visions or heavenly voices, which were the product only of the monk's fevered imagination; instead the mind must become 'naked'.[21]

This kind of apophatic or 'silent' experience is now alien to us – and that is probably one of the reasons that so many people in the West find the concept of God difficult today. We have already met Denys the Areopagite who, until the late Middle Ages, influenced nearly every major Western theologian.[22] His aim was to make all Christians, layfolk as well as monks, conscious of the limitations of language in theology. God, he pointed out, is given fifty-two names in the Bible – he is called a rock and compared to the sky, the sea and so on, but these titles are clearly inadequate because God is obviously *not* a rock. His more sophisticated names, however – Wisdom, Goodness, Unity – are more dangerous because they give us the false impression that we know what God is like: we assume that 'He' is wise, good and unified in the way that we understand these words. Yet God is not 'good' like a good person or a good meal. We must make ourselves aware, therefore, that even the most exalted things we say about God are bound to be misleading. So when we listen to the scriptures during the liturgy, Denys explained, we should reverently deny the names they give to God, finding each one inadequate, and fall into a humbled silence in the presence of the ineffable.

This exercise did not make Denys's congregation feel baffled or thwarted; rather, it brought them into the same kind of reverent, solemn silence that the Aryan priests experienced at the end of the Brahmodya. Everybody, Denys insisted, priests and layfolk alike, should listen to scripture in this way, plunging 'into that darkness that lies beyond intellect', and eventually we would all 'find ourselves not simply running short of words but actually speechless and unknowing'.[23] This was not a dry cerebral exercise but was practised in the heightened and emotive drama of the Byzantine liturgy with evocative music, stylised drama and clouds of incense which, like any great aesthetic experience, touched people emotionally, stirring them at a deeper level of their being. As the congregation listened to the words of scripture, intoned in a special chant that separated them from ordinary discourse, they learned at a level deeper than logos that what we call 'God' is not *this* or *that* but something immeasurably 'other'. He was qaddosh – the Hebrew word meaning 'holy' and 'apart'. The liturgy had initiated the congregation into a different mode of being and seeing. They would have understood what Job felt when, at the end of God's passionate speech, he touched his lips and fell silent.

So, like the Brahman and the Dao, what we call God lies beyond the reach of reason. But significantly, Job came to see this not by a dramatic vision like Isaiah's nor by elaborate theological discourse, but by a divinely revealed insight into the sacrality of nature. He learned that, like God, nature was holy, *tremendum et fascinans*. In other traditions, as we have seen, the divine and nature had always been inseparable but for Job, the Israelite, this was a novel insight.

For us today in the West too it is an unfamiliar idea. Since the fourteenth century, we have built an entirely different notion of the sacred. By rationalising nature and confining God to the heavens, we have so drastically reduced the divine that for many it has become either incredible or imperceptible. At the same time, in our industrialised societies, we have been systematically destroying the natural order. By forcing the natural world to upgrade our lives and failing to see its essential holiness, we have damaged it perhaps irreparably. At the same time, by excluding a reverence for nature from our conception of the divine, we have developed an unnatural perception of God. Unlike other scriptures, the Bible itself has encouraged this, suggesting that nature is subordinate to Yahweh and subservient to our needs. But the unknown author of Job is a prophet for our time bringing us an urgent message. He tells us that when we look at the natural world, we can no longer regard it simply as a resource. Instead, like Job, we must learn to appreciate its mystery, and cry, 'Holy! Holy! Holy!'

4

Our Broken World

Almost every time we listen to the evening news, we are inundated with accounts of tragedy, sorrow and cruelty. Despite our extraordinary technological achievements, we seem unable to assuage the poverty, suffering and injustice that afflicts swathes of humanity. All too often we push these unpleasant truths to the back of our minds. When the newscaster introduces some particularly upsetting footage these days, she is obliged to alert the audience – 'A warning: you may find the next item distressing' – giving us an opportunity to switch channels or go and make a cup of tea to avoid the disturbing sight.

Traditionally, however, religion devised stories and rituals that compelled people to look unflinchingly at the inherent sorrow of life. In India, some creation myths suggested that our world was deeply flawed and broken from the very beginning. These were very different from the optimistic creation story in Genesis, where God was convinced that everything was 'good'. The Indian creator god, Prajapati ('the All'), was a personification of the Brahman. In the texts of the *Rig Veda*, the earliest of the Indian scriptures, he had been the force that sustained the universe and planted the seed of consciousness in the human mind. Prajapati, we are told, had produced the creative heat known as *tapas* from within himself which enabled him to bring the tripartite universe, consisting of earth, sky and heaven, into existence. He then 're-entered' the universe, so that he became its divine breath and very being. The world was therefore quintessentially divine, infused with the sacred. But in the *Brahmanas*, a collection of priestly texts dating from the ninth century BCE, the creation story became more disturbing.

In these darker tales, Prajapati no longer created the universe effortlessly. The intense strain of igniting tapas caused his body to explode and its fractured pieces became the tripartite universe and the essence of the devas as well as all the creatures that inhabited the earth.[1] It was a catastrophe. 'Truly,' wrote the priest author, 'there was no firm foundation' of the world.[2] Prajapati's creatures were weak and sickly: some could not breathe and others were tormented by demons; they fought and ate one another. Prajapati was so enfeebled by his exertions that he had to be revived by the very gods he had created.[3] Emptied of his life force and terrified of death, he begged Agni, the sacred fire, to put his body back together again.[4] So Agni built him up, piece by piece, and his restoration was re-enacted by the Vedic priest in the daily ritual of constructing the fire altar:

> The same Prajapati who became broken is this very fire we now build [on the altar]. That very fire-pan over there which lies empty before being retracted is just like Prajapati as he lay collapsed . . . He [the priest] warms [the empty pot] on the fire, just as the gods once warmed [Prajapati].[5]

The story of Prajapati is a myth that, enacted and enlivened by ritual, revealed a profound truth that is only too evident to us today: we live in a potentially broken world. In India, this grim teaching was imparted not in the abstract, scientific terms of modern environmentalism, but in a narrative that was brought to life by the imaginative artistry of ritual. Even though, unlike us, the Aryans were not responsible for their damaged world, they felt obliged to repair it and make it safe for themselves. Every day, when they constructed the fire altar, the priests symbolically reconstructed the damaged cosmos. It 'should measure the distance of the outstretched arms' and depict a man's body. Two offertory vessels represented Prajapati's hands; two milk pots, his ears; two pieces of gold, his eyes. Morning and evening, the priest kindled sticks to supply him with food. 'These same acts should be performed throughout the whole year . . . unless he [the priest] wants to see our father Prajapati torn apart.'[6]

> Whatever fire there is in this world is [Prajapati's] inward breath; the atmosphere is his body; whatever winds there may be are his body's vital breath. The sky is his head, the sun and moon are his eyes . . . Now that same firm foundation which the gods put together is here, even today and will be so hereafter.[7]

Enacted daily in the drama of ritual, and accompanied by the emotive chanting of the sacred mantras and the inspired poetry of the rishis, a concern for the fragility of their world became part of the Aryans' consciousness. They learned that nature was vulnerable and that it was up to humans to revere and rescue it every day.[8] The ritual was not just a re-enactment of Prajapati's story but also a reminder of their responsibility to heal and nurture their compromised world. Crucially, its aesthetic power enabled participants to glimpse the inherent sacrality of the 'luminous pure world' that they feared they were losing.[9]

There was, therefore, a deliberate evocation of grief for the damaged world at the heart of Aryan religion. For Muslims, reciting the Qur'an fulfils a similar purpose and has an emotional force like the chanting of Indian mantras. This is difficult for non-Muslims to appreciate, because the extraordinary poignancy of the Arabic does not come across in translation and they simply read the text instead of hearing it recited. The first Muslims were astounded, even shocked, by the beauty of the Qur'an, which was so unlike traditional Arabic poetry. Emotionally transported, some 'fell to their knees and wept'. The recitation caused their skins 'to quiver . . . and their hearts to soften', and their eyes were 'overflowing with tears because they recognize the truth [in it]'.[10] While Christians encounter the Word of God in Jesus, for Muslims, the Divine Word is present in the sound of the Qur'anic text that is recited in communal worship. When they learn it by heart, they imbibe it in an act of holy communion.

Qur'anic recitation is a major art form in the Islamic

world. The chant evokes a state known as *huzn*, meaning 'sorrow', 'grief' or 'plaintiveness', and it arouses powerful feelings for the pain of human life. Music, as the philosopher Susanne Langer (1895–1985) explained, can evoke 'emotions and moods we have not felt, passions we did not know before'.[11] Similarly huzn evokes feelings of 'true humility, awe of the divine, human frailty and mortality'.[12] Sorrow and the empathy that feeds our sense of justice are deeply connected.[13] Indeed, neurophysicists tell us that aesthetic experience is more effective in arousing an appreciation of suffering than a more objective, cognitive approach;[14] it may, therefore, elicit an empathy with the pain of nature that more cerebral or scientific accounts of our environmental crisis cannot.

The great Muslim mystic Muid ad-Din ibn al-Arabi (1165–1240) based his theology on an ancient *hadith* ('tradition') in Islam which is said to have recorded the words of God: 'I was a hidden treasure, and I desired to be known. Accordingly I created the creatures and thereby made myself known to them. And they did come to know Me.' Because the Absolute was mysteriously hidden even from itself, Ibn al-Arabi explained, it experienced a yearning to know itself and become known, which impelled it to step out of the abysmal darkness of non-being and become manifest.[15] This 'holy emanation' began in indescribable pain, an inchoate wrench that stirred deeply within the Absolute. It emitted a sigh of sorrow and compassion for all the incipient beings coming into existence, which Ibn al-Arabi described in a forceful image: when we hold our breath for a considerable length of time, it becomes unbearably painful and can erupt in an explosive exhalation or a sob. Sorrow, therefore, is not confined to humankind; it lies in the depths of the divine and is the foundation of all things.[16]

In another hadith, attributed to the prophet Muhammad, it is said that this sigh became a cloud (*amū*): 'Someone asked the Prophet: Where was your Lord before creating His [visible] Creation? Muhammad replied: "He was in the Cloud; there was no space either above or below." '[17] The cloud was a divine emanation in which the hidden Absolute revealed its inner self and assumed a 'thingness', a vaporous, tentative existence. Later, this cloud would conceive and give form to all the things of creation. Thus creation comes from a manifestation within the divine of a yearning to be known, and the explosive sob, which started the creation process, lies within every being in the cosmos. 'The world and everything in it becomes manifest in the breath of the All-Merciful,' Ibn al-Arabi tells us. When God says in the Qur'an, 'My Mercy embraces all things,'[18] he tells us that he is incarnate in everything and every person. But the creative sigh did not happen just once in an abysmal past. Rather, in a way that is strikingly similar to the Daoist vision of reality, it continues ceaselessly in the constant overflow of the Absolute into its creation and thus keeps the world in existence. So for Ibn al-Arabi, the natural world *is* the 'breath of the Merciful' and everything in it is an expression of the divine sigh.

A later Jewish creation myth also reflects a broken world. When the Jews of Spain were evicted from the Iberian Peninsula by the Catholic monarchs Ferdinand and Isabella in 1492, they experienced spiritual as well as physical dislocation. Their old world had been swept away and the exiles could no longer make sense of their lives. They found that traditional Judaism no longer spoke to them. Those who took refuge in Palestine in the Ottoman Empire settled in Safed in Galilee, convinced that when the Messiah came, they would be the first to greet him there. Some believed that they found him in the saintly Isaac Luria (1534–72). Luria told a creation story that bore no relation to the Genesis account but illuminated the broken world of Jews who were still reeling from the shock of deportation and made their lives not only tolerable but joyous.

The story begins with an act of voluntary exile. Luria asked how the world could exist if God was omnipresent, filling all the available space with his divine self. The answer was *Zimzum* ('withdrawal'): the infinite and inaccessible Godhead – which the Kabbalists called En Sof – shrank to evacuate a region within itself to make room for the world. In a way, God was inflicting an exile upon a part of itself. What's more, unlike the orderly Genesis myth, Luria's creation was a violent process of primal explosions, disasters and expulsions which seemed to the Sephardic exiles a far more accurate reflection of their world. At first, En Sof had tried to fill the emptiness it had created by Zimzum with divine light, but the 'vessels' and 'pipes' that contained the light shattered under the strain. So sparks of this sacred light fell into the abyss that was not God. After this disaster, creation was awry; everything was in the wrong place and the Shekhinah, the presence that is the closest we come to an apprehension of the divine on earth, wandered through the world in perpetual exile, yearning to be reunited with the Godhead – a clear reflection of the world of the Jewish exiles that seemed irrevocably broken.[19]

Luria's followers invented rites that enabled them to partake in the divine discomfort that infused the whole world. They would lie awake at night calling out to God like lovers, lamenting the pain of separation that lies at the heart of so much human distress.

They would take long walks in the countryside, wandering like the Shekhinah in exile. But Luria was adamant that there must be no self-indulgent wallowing. The midnight rites always ended at dawn with a meditation on the final reunion of the Shekhinah with the Godhead. And, Luria insisted, Jews who had suffered ostracism must behave compassionately: there were penances for harming or humiliating others.

The Way Forward

In this chapter, we have explored some creation myths that are very different from the serene story recounted in the first chapter of Genesis, where there is no pain or struggle and God simply utters six commands that bring the world dutifully into being. In the myths we have just considered, we learn that sorrow, pain and even self-harm lie at the heart of creation. Prajapati's creation is a mess: he blows himself up in the process and has to plead with the gods (whom he has created) to put him back together again. His creatures, the *Brahmanas* tell us, are drastically enfeebled: some run away from him in terror; others are created misshapen, blind, impotent and badly damaged. We can only speculate on what inspired this vision of a radically broken world. At the time the Aryans were extending their territory and would soon establish powerful kingdoms in the Ganges Basin, but they clearly felt that they were living in a compromised world. We can share this anxiety as we survey the injury that we ourselves have inflicted on our natural environment – and on one another.

Perhaps we should make ourselves feel more disturbed, spending some time each day to reflect on the pain being inflicted on both our fellow humans and the environment, considering the broken lives in war-torn Yemen or Somalia, the widespread poverty in Africa, and the desperate plight of the Rohingya Muslims and people of Ukraine. Nearly every day, migrants risk death by crossing the English Channel in inadequate boats, hoping to find refuge in the United Kingdom, and some are drowning in the attempt. Why are we not more distressed by the shameful inequity of some of our rich cities? London, where I live, is one of the richest in the world, yet it is estimated that a quarter of its population live in poverty. In the United States, there is a wider disparity between rich and poor than in any other developed nation, and over the last few decades, this wealth gap has more than doubled.[20] And how long will it take us to eradicate the racism that still poisons our societies, protests against which erupted so vehemently throughout the world after the murder of

George Floyd? These questions should not only trouble us but impel us to thoughtful and dedicated action.

Religious traditions ask us to reflect seriously on the pain of the world. Today we often expect religion to bring us peace of mind and happiness – 'tidings of comfort and of joy', as the Christmas carol has it. Indeed, the Christmas story itself tends to be prettified, presenting the Christ child in a cosy stable with a benign and clean-looking ox and ass. Yet the gospels of Matthew and Luke present a harsher picture: the Messiah was born in a hovel and becomes a refugee. The sorrow at the heart of the world is dramatically expressed in Ibn al-Arabi's description of the convulsive sob at the root of God's self-revelation. Religion calls us to be ever mindful of it in a way that does not depress or overwhelm us but elicits compassion, the ability to feel with the other – even, as Jesus reminded us, our enemies. Because compassion frees us from the prison of our ego, it enables us to experience the otherness – the holiness – of what we call God.

But, of course, the suffering that we witness should afflict us all, whatever our beliefs or lack of them. We need to dwell on these images of pain and allow them to disturb us. Only thus can we elicit the compassion – the ability to 'feel with' others – that inspires constructive action.

5

Sacrifice

Animal sacrifice was central to ancient religion. Today we regard it as cruel and barbaric, but our ancestors would be equally, if not more, horrified by the casual butchering of millions of beasts in our abattoirs every day. In the ancient world, people did not usually eat meat unless it had been ritually slaughtered. Sacrifice was designed to transform all its participants – including the animal victim – with demanding religious ceremonies that took a remarkably similar form around the world.

A great deal of what we know about sacrificial rites comes from India. Originally, when the Aryans were still nomads herding their cattle, their sacrifices had been raucous affairs. Because the wealth of their society was regarded as a gift from the gods, the ritual was designed to ensure further divine aid: the gods would receive the choicest portions of the animal, which Agni, the sacred fire, conveyed to heaven. Afterwards, there was a riotous banquet, followed by mock raids, rowdy competitions and shooting matches.

But by the ninth century BCE, the Brahmin priests had embarked on a reform that systematically extracted much of the violence from the ritual. Now the sacrificer – normally the patron who sponsored the ceremony – was the only layman present in the ritual arena, where four priests guided him through the ceremony. The old rowdy contests had been replaced by anodyne chants and elaborate symbolic gestures. There was also an entirely new concern for the welfare of the animal. Indeed, the *Brahmanas* frankly condemned animal sacrifice as cruel, recommending that, if possible, the beast be spared at the last moment and donated to one of the officiating priests. But if it had to be killed, they insisted, it must be dispatched as painlessly and with as much dignity as possible.

These reformed rituals focused on the sacrificer's inner world. In the old rites, he had simply inflicted death on the animal victim; in the new ceremony he was instructed to assimilate its death symbolically, experiencing the whole process internally in a ritualised journey to heaven. But the sacrifice now required intensive preparation. The sacrificer had to understand how every single ritualised action, liturgical utensil or chanted hymn was connected to a particular divine reality. So before he could even set foot in the sacrificial arena, he had to undergo a series of demanding rituals that were designed to transform him: because he was about to make a journey to heaven, he had to be temporarily divinised. This was a process that could take weeks or even months.[1] The sacrificer had to live in a specially built hut carefully segregated from the profane world. He was shaved and had his hair and nails cut in the style of the gods. He was ritually cleansed in a purifying bath and donned a linen garment that marked the beginning of his life as a deity.[2] In order to be reborn as a god, he had first to become a foetus: his head was veiled to resemble the foetus's cowl, and he had to clench his fists and walk in a way that resembled its movements in the womb. Finally, when he was considered ready for the next step, he was reborn. Now that the patron had become a god, he was allowed no contact with impure castes; he could not be touched, and he was permitted to drink nothing but milk until he was ready for his ritualised journey to heaven.

On the day of the ceremony, the sacrificer became one with Prajapati, the creator God who had performed the very first sacrifice. Re-enacting Prajapati's sacrifice, he abandoned the profane world of mortality and entered the divine order. He could therefore declare: 'I have attained heaven, the gods; I am become immortal!' But it was not just a matter of going through performative rites. All these links between the patron and the gods, between heaven and earth, were forged by means of an intensive mental effort. It was a ritualised *yoga*, a 'yoking' together of different realities.[3]

If the animal victim was not spared at the last minute, it was ritually bathed and asked formally if it consented to the sacrifice. It was addressed with extreme courtesy, ceremonially praised and exhorted to keep calm. Finally, it was tied to the stake. It was given water to drink and bathed again, and its head was anointed with butter. Finally the priest representing Agni would pluck a brand from the fire and walk three times around the animal, consecrating the victim and setting it apart from the attendants as befitted its sacred status. The divinised sacrificer would embrace the victim because it was now one with both him and the gods. In the old rites he had been able to pass the guilt of the animal's death on to the other participants but now, by symbolically becoming one with the sacrificed animal, he took its death into his own being; and by offering himself to the gods, he believed that – like the animal – he would experience immortality. 'Becoming himself the sacrifice,' the *Brahmanas* explained, 'the sacrificer frees himself from death.'[4]

As the dreaded moment approached, the animal's pardon was asked for and the other members of its species were begged not to take revenge. It was gently placed in the correct position, and everyone fell silent. The officiating priest turned away, uttering propitiatory mantras, and then gave orders to the sacrificer, who tightened the noose around the animal's neck until its spirit departed.

After the slaughter, the victim, now liberated from the profane world, was sanctified. Its lifeless body was believed to be filled with a holy force and it was treated with great respect. It was then dismembered and its remains laid on the altar. Special portions were reserved for the gods, while the rest was distributed to all those who had participated in the ceremony. Everyone was then methodically desacralised so that they could return safely to the profane world. The four priests, the sacrificer and his wife purified each other by a ritualised washing of hands before putting on new clothes, thereby resuming their secular identity.

The sacrifice was in part an attempt to look unflinchingly at the fate of an animal destined to be consumed and imbue it with as much dignity as possible. But at the heart of it is a central paradox: an enhanced life comes from a ritually sacralised death. A very late hymn in the *Rig Veda* suggests that the world in all its multiplicity came from the self-sacrifice of a single god. We are told that Purusha, the divine 'Person', was the source of 'all that is, all that ever was, and all that ever will be'. Not only was he the lord of heaven and earth but he was present in all beings: 'he spreads out in all directions, into both animate and inanimate things'. The hymn describes Purusha walking calmly into the sacrificial arena, lying down on the freshly strewn grass, and allowing the gods to kill him in an immolation that sets the cosmos in motion. Indeed, Purusha *was* the universe, which was itself therefore sacred. Everything that exists was generated from his corpse – heaven and earth, sun and moon, animals and humans. So were the four classes of Vedic society:

> His mouth became the Brahmin; his arms were made into the Warrior; his thighs the people and from his feet the Servants were born.[5]

In later traditions, Purusha would merge with Prajapati, and finally he would become the Brahman, the ultimate reality.

The Indian myths tell us that it was not domination, power or aggression that created the world: creation and indeed creativity itself result from *kenosis* – the purging of ego. But how do we abandon our selves? We have seen how the Aryan priests ritually re-enacted the story of Prajapati by building up the fire altar every day and symbolically reconstructing his body and our world. But only a small part of the Aryan population could participate in these elaborate rites, so for ordinary people the priests devised devotions known as *pañcamahāyajñas*, the 'Five Great Sacrifices'. These were simple practices that could be performed by anyone at any time.[6] They became central to Hindu life and enabled people to develop habitual attitudes of compassion, gratitude and practical concern for their fellow humans and the natural world.[7] First, they daily placed a small bowl of food outside for hungry or sick animals.[8] Second, all guests, invited or uninvited, had to be welcomed and honoured as if they were gods and fed until they could eat no more.[9] The third and fourth rituals ensured that both the deceased and the devas were remembered with love and reverence every day, with simple offerings of rice, grains or fruit thrown into the family's fire. The final ritual was the daily study of scripture, which simply involved reciting a hymn softly to concentrate the mind, while sitting cross-legged in a quiet place, with eyes either closed or fixed on the horizon.

The Way Forward

This chapter reminds us that religion is hard work. Its rituals are designed to effect a profound change within us. A religious ritual should be a transformative event – it can never be a matter of simply going through the motions, however piously. Holiness demands that we change our lives and, indeed, our very selves. The sacrificer spent months in an uncomfortable hut, undergoing demanding and uncomfortable rites before he was permitted to perform the temple sacrifice, which itself required intense concentration. The rituals challenged participants at a profound level, insisting that in some way the rites properly observed would change their minds.

This is not what most of us associate with religious ritual, which we often experience as something familiar, consoling and undemanding. But it is what is required of us as we face our current environmental crisis. We must re-form our attitude to nature and that will entail sacrifice. We can no longer board aeroplanes, drive our cars, or burn coal with our former insouciance. If we want a viable world, we must awaken within ourselves a new reverence for nature, just as the sacrificer learned to regard an unremarkable sheep as sacred. We cannot save our planet unless we undergo a radical change of mind and heart, which will inevitably be demanding. This transformation cannot take place overnight. We too have to learn to see the things of nature with reverence, and this will require sustained effort, an authentic change of heart, discipline and commitment.

The 'Five Great Sacrifices' seem far removed from the grandiose sacrificial dramas that we have considered in this chapter. But they point to something important and inherent in the whole concept of sacrifice. Our word 'sacrifice' comes from the Latin *sacrificium*, which means 'to make holy', and shares an even older Latin ancestor with our word 'sacred'. 'Sacrifice', therefore, doesn't merely refer to the slaughter of the victim; its literal meaning is to sanctify, to make holy. The emphasis is on the consecration or divinisation of an object, animal or person. Hindus were taught to regard a perfectly ordinary visitor – any visitor – as sacred and to honour them as if they were divine. And, indeed, in the elaborate dramas that we have just considered, the death of the animal victim is rather an anticlimax: it came only after the beast had been ritually honoured as a sacred being and become so holy that none of the priests dared address it directly. Similarly, far more time and effort was spent on the transformation of the patron into a divinity than on his final slaughter of the animal.

Perhaps we should create our own 'Five Great Sacrifices' and build them into our daily lives. Every day we should try to honour in our minds the holiness of every single natural object and person that we encounter. Every day, we will probably fail; but each time we should try and start again, knowing that each person we come across is a holy mystery and that each animal or plant has its own unique dignity and beauty. All must be treated with kindness and reverence.

6

Kenosis

The story of Purusha walking calmly into the sacrificial arena and allowing the gods to kill him, thus enabling the cosmos to arise, is a classic expression of what the Greeks called kenosis, an 'emptying' of self. From a very early period, kenosis was regarded as crucial not only to people's spiritual life but to the entire world order. However, abandoning our ego is not a popular virtue in the modern world. On the contrary, we seem to value self-assertion as a sign of strength, courage and intelligence in our politicians, businessmen and even our religious leaders. Environmentalists also resort to angry posturing and even violence in their zeal to save us from ecological catastrophe. It is true, though, that we value kenosis when we see it in certain popular figures such as Mahatma Gandhi, Martin Luther King and Nelson Mandela. Kenosis, properly understood, liberates us from the destructive strictures and blindness of egotism. It opens up a new understanding of ourselves and a fresh perception of the world around us.

The first chapter of the Book of Genesis depicts Yahweh, the God of Israel, as a benevolent creator. He does not have to fight fearful battles to bring the cosmos into being but is in total command of his creation. He blesses everything he has made and declares it to be 'good'. This cosmogony was probably composed by those Israelites who had been deported to Babylonia after the destruction of Jerusalem and its temple in the late sixth century BCE. Here every year they would have witnessed the ritual processions that celebrated the creation of the world by the Mesopotamian god Marduk after he had fought a series of battles with other monstrous deities. Their god, Yahweh, the Israelites claimed defiantly, was far more powerful. He only had to utter a few words to create the universe.

But this story is very different from the other cosmologies we have discussed, where creation is not attributed to an extrinsic divine power but understood as a dynamic force working tirelessly and subtly within everything. Elsewhere people contemplated a cosmos in which every being – human, animal, vegetable, mineral – participated harmoniously in a mysterious, self-generating process.[1] Instead of a Darwinian nature red in tooth and claw, the result of endless competition for dominance, we encounter a never-ending kenosis in which everything creatively and spontaneously 'yields' to one another. In India, the devas, after bringing the cosmos into being, did not depart from the natural world to heaven, where they could observe events on earth from a lofty, superior position. They resided in the things they had created, 'entering the world through their hidden natures'.

Kenosis is abundantly evident in the Dao which, Laozi explains, infuses the whole natural world with a dynamic that enables each individual 'thing' to become itself. This creative power applies no force. It

> gives them life yet claims no possession;
> It benefits them yet exacts no gratitude;
> It is the steward yet exercises no authority.
> Such is called the mysterious virtue (de).[2]

The sage deliberately aligns himself with nature in a continuous kenosis:

In accordance with this, the sacred man puts
himself in the rear and therefore comes
naturally to the fore.
He remains outside, and because of that he is
always there.
Is it not because he possesses no ego that he
can thus establish his Self?[3]

Instead of governing by force, it is its apparent weakness that makes the Dao so effective. Similarly, the sage is the perfect man, who personifies the Dao because he has eradicated all traces of ego:

Therefore the sage embraces the One and is a
model for all things under Heaven.
He does not show himself, and so is
conspicuous;
He does not consider himself right, and so is
illustrious;
He does not brag, and so has merit;
He does not boast and so endures;
It is because he does not contend that no one in
the world is in a position to contend with him.[4]

Whereas reason can make us arrogant and inflexible, and desire can make us aggressive and selfish, the Daoist ideal is that we abandon our ego and imitate the kenosis that manifests itself in the natural world. We then find that kenosis is empowering because it aligns us with the way things truly are instead of putting us at loggerheads with them. Having no ego does not mean that the sage has no emotions; he experiences anger and sorrow like everybody else, but there is something imperturbable at his core that gives him mysterious power.

But how can we reach this inner state of selflessness? The Buddha advocated a practice he called *anatta* ('no-self'), which enabled many of his disciples to achieve enlightenment. He told them to notice how their feelings were often in flux, careening from one extreme to another. Desires and fears course through our minds but tend to evaporate quickly. Our desires come and go: what seemed crucial yesterday no longer seems so urgent today. So if we are being honest with ourselves, we have to admit: 'This is not me; this is not what I really am; this is not myself.'[5] The Buddha liked to compare what we call personality to a blazing fire or a rushing stream: it has some kind of form but the parts change from one moment to the next. He compared the human mind to a monkey ranging through the forest, grabbing one branch, letting it go and then seizing another. He told his monks that if they sit back and observe these mood swings calmly they will begin to see how ephemeral they truly are.

The Buddha was not presenting his disciples with complex philosophical insight or neurological evidence. This was a practical call to action, which many people have found helpful ever since. He suggested that we should behave *as if* the ego did not exist. Dwelling on the self leads to selfish notions about 'me' and 'mine' and unhelpful states of mind – jealousy, conceit, megalomania, pride, even violence. That greedy, frightened ego does much harm, to others as well as ourselves. When the Buddha first explained the concept of anatta to five monks at the beginning of his teaching, they responded with relief and delight. They tried to live *as if* the self did not exist and found that they were happier. Living beyond concerns about status, needs and desires can be liberating. We feel a lot better for it; we enter a richer, fuller mode of existence. This cannot be verified empirically; the only way of discovering the truth of anatta is to put it into practice.

From the very earliest days of Christianity, it seems that kenosis was central to understanding Jesus's life and death. Writing some twenty-five years after Jesus's crucifixion, St Paul quoted an early

Christian hymn in a letter to his converts in Philippi. While Jesus had embodied the divine nature, he told them, he had taken no pride in this:

> but emptied himself (*heauton ekenosen*)
> to assume the condition of a slave . . .
> and being as all men are,
> he was humbler yet, even to accepting death,
> death on a cross.[6]

It was because of his self-effacing acceptance of this brutal death that God had raised Jesus to the highest heaven, bestowing upon him the supreme title of *Kyrios* ('Lord'). Here Paul was not instructing the Philippians in the Christian doctrine of redemption, which would be formulated much later. This was not a theological doctrine but a truth that would make sense to the Philippians only if they practised kenosis in their own lives. 'In your minds,' St Paul told them, 'you must be the same as Christ Jesus.' They too must empty their minds of egotism, selfishness and pride and be united in love, 'with a common purpose and a common mind'.[7]

> There is to be no competition among you, no conceit; but everybody is to be self-effacing.

> Always consider the other person to be better than yourself, so that nobody thinks of his own interests first, but everybody thinks of other people's interests instead.[8]

Only if they revered and served others in this selfless way would the Philippians understand the meaning of Jesus's kenosis and experience an enhanced life as 'sons of God' themselves. Later Christians would set much store by orthodoxy and the acceptance of correct teaching, but for Paul religion was about kenosis and love. You might have faith that could move mountains, he told his readers, but without love, which requires the constant transcendence of egotism, it is worthless. 'Love is . . . never boastful or conceited; it is never rude or selfish; it does not take offence and is not resentful.'[9] Instead of clinging desperately to an inflated sense of self, love was 'empty' – kenotic – and endlessly respectful of others.

The four gospels, written between 70 and 110 CE, were all, in different ways, influenced by Paul. They depict Jesus reaching out in love towards prostitutes, lepers, epileptics and those who collected the hated Roman taxes. The people who would be able to enter the kingdom of God were those who practised compassion, fed the hungry and visited the sick and incarcerated. Jesus even commanded his followers to love their enemies:

> For if you love those who love you, how can you claim any credit? Even the tax-collectors and the pagans do as much, do they not? And if you save your greetings for your brothers, are you doing anything exceptional? You must be perfect as your heavenly father is perfect.[10]

The paradox 'Love your enemies' requires the most radical kenosis of all. We are told to offer benevolence where there is little or no hope of any return.

In the seventh century CE the prophet Muhammad brought the Qur'an, a divinely inspired scripture, to the people of the Hijaz, his birthplace in the western Arabian Peninsula. The Qur'an did not claim to be a new divine revelation but simply restated the message God had given to prophets of the past, before the one true religion had split into rival sects. One of the key Muslim virtues was kenosis. The desert Arabs of the Hijaz were a self-sufficient, proud and chauvinistic people, but for some years before he received the revelations that would be recorded in the Qur'an, Muhammad and his wife Khadija made an annual retreat to Mount Hira, just outside Mecca, where he distributed alms to the poor and performed devotional rituals that included deep prostrations before Allah.[11] All humans are dependent upon God, their creator, Muhammad told his early followers. Allah wanted them to approach him, but not in a spirit of pride. 'Touch your head to the earth!'[12] God commanded, a posture that would have been anathema to the haughty Meccans.

These revelations brought to light a fault-line in the city, which was abandoning traditional tribal equality as it embraced an aggressive market economy. Muhammad's converts were deeply moved by the exquisite beauty of the new scripture, which urged them to share their wealth fairly instead of building private fortunes. But it was not sufficient simply to work for social reform; without an inner transformation, Muhammad taught, change would only be superficial. They would have to cultivate a kenotic attitude, look after the poor and needy, free their slaves, and perform small acts of kindness numerous times a day, purging their hearts of selfishness and pride.

Most importantly, they must meet for *salat* ('group prayer') at stated times during the day. This interrupted their daily business and helped Muslims to remember that Allah was their first priority. These prayers involved deep prostrations of the body, a practice which was difficult for the arrogant Meccan grandees, who were asked to grovel on the ground like slaves. The word *islam* means 'surrender' and this is first and foremost a surrender of the ego; a *muslim* is a man or woman who has made this existential relinquishment of self. Our bodily movements shape our awareness and perceptions, and these prostrations, practised five times a day, instructed Muslims at a level deeper than the rational to abandon their ego in a daily, hourly kenosis.

The Way Forward

In the modern world we are taught to value our achievements, assert ourselves and our opinions, and constantly promote ourselves, sometimes quite aggressively. And there is value in this. As a young nun in the 1960s, I was repeatedly told to cultivate a habit of humility; we had to kiss the ground as a formal mode of apology and were endlessly berated in public on our many failings. But this was not kenosis, an 'emptying' of self, because instead of forgetting ourselves we became neurotically self-conscious: we were perversely embedded in the ego that we were supposed to transcend.

The ancient creation myths that we have discussed suggest that kenosis lies at the heart of the world order and that it is the core of true spirituality. Zhuangzi tells the story of Yan Hui, who informed his teacher Confucius that he was making progress in his spiritual development. 'How come?' Confucius asked. Because, Yan Hui replied, he had forgotten everything that the master had taught him, about ritual and music, benevolence and righteousness. Not only that, he claimed, 'I can sit down and forget *everything* . . . I let my body fall away and the intellect fail; I throw out form and abandon understanding – and then move away freely, blending away into qi.'[13] 'If you blend away like that, you're free of likes and dislikes,' Confucius exclaimed in astonishment. 'So in the end, the true sage here is you! So you won't mind if I follow you from now on.' While Confucius declared that Yan Hui had surpassed him, his humility shows that he too was practising kenosis and was well on the road to sagehood.

Whereas Daoists saw kenosis as the source of true power, we often seek the direct opposite. We specialise in serving ourselves and in the process, we impose our will on others and on nature, often with terrible results. Many of us are eager to achieve spiritual enlightenment of some kind but often we don't realise that this entails the loss of the self that we so busily and inventively preserve and promote. The Buddha realised this shortly before he achieved Nirvana, when he recalled a moment from his early childhood that had given him intimations of another mode of being. His father had taken him to watch the ceremonial ploughing of the fields before the planting of the new crops and left him under the supervision of his nurses, but they abandoned him to watch the planting. Finding himself alone, the little boy noticed that during the ploughing, the young grass had been torn up and insects and their eggs had been destroyed. He was filled with a strange sorrow, as though his own relatives had been killed. But it was a beautiful day and a feeling of pure joy rose unbidden in his heart. In this sudden surge of pity, he had experienced an ekstasis – a moment of spontaneous compassion, which took him beyond himself, allowing the pain of lowly, insignificant creatures to pierce him to the heart. Instinctively, without any instruction, the child sat in the yogic position and felt the calm happiness of a trance that was usually accessible only to advanced yogins.

The point of yoga, as originally conceived, was not peace of mind or enhanced concentration. It was kenosis. Chinese philosophers similarly taught their disciples to submit their desires and behaviour to the natural rhythms of life. Hebrew prophets insisted on submission to the will of God in concern for others, and Jesus would tell his followers that the spiritual life demanded the death of the self: a grain of wheat must fall to the ground and die before it bore fruit. Similarly, the sages who devised yoga realised that egotism was the greatest hindrance to an experience of the sacred. Thus yoga can be described as the systematic dismantling of the egotism that distorts our view of the world. Even as a small child, the Buddha instinctively understood what happened when you left the self behind in compassion for other beings – in this case for the insects heartlessly killed during the ploughing of fields. As that day progressed, the shadows of the trees moved but not that of the rose-apple tree, which continued to shade the meditating child from the sun, much to the astonishment of the nurses when they returned. The young Buddha's empathy had taken him to the heart of the yogic experience.

We may not be ready for the radical extirpation of egotism in yoga, a long process that requires expert supervision. But we can practise a simple exercise that will remind us of the kenosis that is central to a fulfilled human life. This is not a prayer. It is simply a short, sharp reminder of the essential frailty of our humanity that enables us to see ourselves realistically and, hopefully, improve. Every day, first thing in the morning and at night, for just a few moments we should consider three things: how little we know; how frequently we fail in kindness to other beings; and how limited are our desires and yearnings, which so often begin and end in our self.

7

Gratitude

In the autumn of 2020, a fascinating exhibition on the culture of the Arctic opened at the British Museum. I was intrigued to find that, despite their appalling climate, the people of the Arctic seemed filled with gratitude towards nature, and their customs and rituals celebrated the harsh seasonal cycle. Strangely enough, I was reminded of the sweltering deserts of Arabia. Nature does not figure prominently in Judaism and Christianity, but in Islam, it is a divine revelation equal to the Qur'an. Indeed, one of the chief objectives of the Qur'an was to awaken within Muslims an awareness of the divine presence in creation.

Each verse of the Quran is called an *ayah*, a 'sign'

of God; but so is every phenomenon of nature. 'Do you not see?' the Qur'an asks insistently, almost incredulously. 'Have you not considered the extraordinary bounty of nature?'[1] This must have seemed bizarre to the first Muslims. When the Qur'an was revealed to Muhammad in the early seventh century, most of the Arabs of the Hijaz had little time for the natural world.[2] The relentlessly harsh climate of Arabia meant that there was never sufficient food to sustain the population, who lived perpetually on the brink of malnutrition. But, remarkably, the Qur'an insists that nature was Allah's prime miracle. Muslims must not take nature for granted; they should make themselves aware of the extraordinary 'signs' of God's concern and compassion that are in evidence every day. 'Let man consider the food he eats!' God demands. 'We pour down abundant water and cause the soil to split open. We make grain grow, and vines, fresh vegetation, olive trees, date palms, luscious gardens, fruits and fodder – all for you and your livestock to enjoy.'[3]

It is difficult for non-Muslims to understand the appeal of the Qur'an, which in translation often seems prosaic, wearingly repetitive and gravely lacking in structure or organised narrative. But the word *qur'ān* itself means 'recitation'. It was scripture designed not to be read privately but to be recited aloud, so the sound of the words was an essential part of their sense. In seventh-century Arabia, poetry was an important art and the Arabs had developed a highly sophisticated critical ear.[4] Yet the language of the Qur'an, the first Muslims noted, was very different from conventional Arabic poetry. They discovered the recurrence of themes, words, phrases and sound patterns – like variations in a piece of music that subtly amplify the original melody and add layer upon layer of complexity. The rich, allusive language and rhythms of the Qur'an help Muslims to slow down their mental processes and enter a different mode of consciousness. It is natural for the congregation to adjust their own breathing to that of the reciter, which not only has a calming effect but helps them to grasp the more elusive teachings of the text. As in yoga, breath control brings a feeling of expansiveness, similar to the effect of music.

In the Qur'an we find once again that religious teachings about nature are imparted aesthetically rather than rationally. We are instructed that wherever we look in the natural world, we find a revelation of the divine: 'The East and the West belong to God; wherever you turn, there is his face. God is all pervading, all knowing.'[5] Muslims must not take nature for granted but regard its rhythms as the self-disclosure of the divine: 'In the succession of night and day, and in what God created in the heavens and earth, there are truly signs (*ayat*) for those who are aware of him.'[6] Muslims are far more impressed by the regular rhythms of nature than by the supernatural miracles celebrated in the Jewish and Christian scriptures, because in the Qur'an the natural order is the revelation of divine power and wisdom. So from a very early date, Muslims advanced the natural sciences, which they regarded as sacred.[7] Indeed, nature itself is the supreme example of *islam*, the wholehearted 'surrender' to the divine that lies at the heart of Muslim spirituality: 'Do you not realise that everything in the heavens and earth submits to God: the sun, the moon, the stars, the mountains, the trees and the animals?'[8] All creatures praise God simply by existing and doing what is ordained for them by nature. They are all, as it were, verses in the sacred book of nature which a devout Muslim learns to read like the poetry of the Qur'anic teachings. In nature we see the ideal *muslim*, someone or something that 'surrenders' wholly to God.

The Qur'an constantly urges Muslims to make themselves aware of God's benevolence in nature.

The natural world is an epiphany that our ordinary modes of thought cannot always perceive. So Muslims must train themselves to see through nature's appearance and glimpse the divine power within. The Qur'an asked Muslims not to abandon their reason and *believe* in the divine presence but to meditate upon the ayat until what had hitherto seemed unremarkable became extraordinary. Muslims are to observe the life force in the regular rhythms of nature and make themselves aware that it is divine: 'It is God who splits the grain and the date-stone, brings forth the living from the dead . . . That then is God.'[9] The invisible forces of nature are sacred. Muslims should note how perfectly the natural rhythms of the cosmos are designed to promote human well-being:

He splits the sky into dawn,
and has made the night for a repose,
and the sun and moon for a reckoning.
That is the ordaining of the
All-mighty, the All-knowing.
It is he who has appointed for you the stars, that
by them you may be guided in
the shadows of land and sea.
We have distinguished the signs (ayat) for
a people who know.[10]

The Qur'an insists that its teachings are addressed to 'a people who know' and 'a people who understand', who deliberately cultivate a sense of wonder for the divine realities of everyday life. This requires continuous practice; a momentary, spontaneous mental uplift is not enough. All the other creatures in our world submit to God's design, the Qur'an insists, and are natural *muslims*. 'The sun runs its course: this is determined by the Almighty, the All-knowing,' God explains, 'and we have determined phases for the moon until finally it becomes like an old date-stalk. The sun cannot overtake the moon, nor can the night outrun the day: each floats in [its own] orbit.'[11] Human beings have the freedom to make a voluntary act of *islam* and to consciously shape their lives so that they reflect the source of being. This is not simply for their personal development; the challenge is to make their society reflect the laws of nature:

> The All-merciful has taught the Qur'an.
> He created man
> and he has taught him the Explanation.
> The sun and the moon to a reckoning,
> and the stars and trees bow themselves
> and the heaven – He raised it up and
> set the Balance.

(Transgress not in the Balance,
and weigh with justice, and skimp
not in the Balance.)
And earth – He set it down for all beings,
therein fruits, and palm-tress with sheaths,
and grain in the blade, and fragrant herbs.
O which of your Lord's bounties will
you and you deny?[12]

Human beings should create societies that reflect the balance that enables the natural world to function harmoniously by acting towards one another with justice and compassion. In the early seventh century, Muhammad's tribe, the Quraysh, were experiencing an economic and social revolution. Their city, Mecca, had become a popular centre for long-distance trade and they themselves had become independent traders. Many were now rich beyond their wildest dreams. Only a few generations earlier, their ancestors had been living precariously in the intractable wilds of northern Arabia, where the terrain was so barren that people could survive only by roaming ceaselessly in search of water, and by fighting endlessly with other tribes for pastureland and grazing rights. But nomadic life had at least been characterised by equity: the tribe could survive only if its meagre resources were shared fairly. But in Mecca, the old communal spirit had been torn apart by a market economy which – as we know only too well – encouraged ruthless competition, greed and individual enterprise. Instead of sharing their wealth fairly, some of the Quraysh were building private fortunes at the expense of the less fortunate.

By the time Muhammad began to receive the revelations that would become the Qur'an, he was gravely troubled by Mecca's social decay. In the Qur'an, the most recent of the scriptures we have considered in this book, we find a close alliance of the two major concerns of religion: the reverence for nature of the Eastern traditions and the monotheistic concern for compassion and equity. Each recitation of the Qur'an must begin with the invocation: 'In the name of God (*al-Lah*), the Compassionate (*al-Rahman*), the Merciful (*al-Rahim*).' Muhammad's religion would eventually be known as 'Islam', the existential 'surrender' that each Muslim must make to God, but it seems that at first it was known as *tazaqqa*, an obscure word that is not easy to translate and perhaps best rendered as 'refinement'. By cultivating tazaqqa, Muslims cloaked themselves in the virtues of compassion and generosity. By giving a proportion of their income in alms (*zakat*) to the poor, fasting during Ramadan to learn what it is like to be hungry, and pondering the dynamic and lessons of nature, they would acquire a spiritual 'refinement'. Tazaqqa was also cultivated in a ritualised action: five times a day, Muslims interrupted their activities for salat; at the sound of the muezzin, they turned in the direction of Mecca and, reciting verses from the Qur'an, prostrated themselves to symbolise their surrender to God. These physical actions transposed to the spiritual, teaching them to lay aside instinctive self-regard.

We should note that the Christian notion of the Last Judgement was central to the early message of the Qur'an. The successful Quraysh no longer felt accountable for their actions, had little concern for the poorer members of their tribe and had acquired an attitude that the Qur'an calls *istighna*, a haughty individualism that we see in our modern societies as well. Later tradition would elaborate on the themes of heaven, hell and judgement, but the Qur'an is more reticent, its language elusive, making it clear that the day of reckoning (*yawm al-din*) was not an event in the distant future but occurred in the here and now. What's more, God is not booming instructions from on high; the Qur'an poses many of its teachings gently in questions: 'Have you not heard?'

'Do you not consider?' People are told to become self-aware and to cultivate *taqwa* ('mindfulness'), which is different from the Buddhist practice: it is an awareness of the lessons of nature and a deep concern for the well-being of others.

The bed-rock message of the Qur'an is that it is wrong to build a private fortune and good to share your wealth with the weak and vulnerable. At life's end, all that would matter was a person's conduct: 'Whoever does a mote's weight good will see it; whoever does a mote's weight wrong will see it.'[13] In the end, deeds that had seemed unimportant would prove to have been momentous. A tiny act of selfishness and unkindness, or, conversely, a spontaneous act of generosity, would become the measure of a human life: 'To free a slave, to feed the destitute on a day of hunger, a kinsman, orphan, or a stranger out of luck, in need.'[14] Muslims must be continually on their guard against selfishness, greed and arrogance. Yet instead of frightening themselves with images of hell, they should meditate on the ayat of God's generosity in the natural world and, with gratitude, aspire to his benevolence.

Look at the camel
  how it is created
Look at the sky and how it is raised

Look at the mountains and how they are set
Look at the earth and how it is spread.[15]

The beauty of the Qur'an, which like all great poetry is lost in translation, calls our attention to the importance of the aesthetic. We have seen throughout this book that important truths are often not imparted in the precise language of logos. For Western readers, a poem written by St Francis of Assisi (d. 1226) offers a powerful example. He wrote it after recovering from a severe illness and, whatever one's beliefs, it is a beautiful meditation on the natural world. We may take the 'Lord' addressed throughout to be the transcendent force that imbues the whole natural order, which some traditions call 'God' but others know as the Dao, the Brahman or Rta.

Most High, all powerful, good Lord
Yours are the praises, the glory, the honour
  and all blessing.

To you, alone, most High, do they belong,
and no man is worthy to mention your name.

Be praised, my Lord, through all your creatures,
especially through my Lord, Brother Sun,

who brings the day and you give light through him.
And he is beautiful and radiant in all his splendour!
of you, Most High, he bears the likeness.

Praised be You, my Lord, through Sister Moon and the stars,
in heaven you formed them clear and precious and beautiful.

Praised be You, my Lord, through Brother Wind,
and through the air, cloudy and serene,
and every kind of weather through which
You give sustenance to your creatures.

Praised be You, my lord, through Sister Water,
which is very useful and humble and precious and chaste.

Praised be You, my Lord, through Brother Fire,
through whom you light the night and he is beautiful
and playful and robust and strong.

Praised be You, my Lord,
through those who give pardon for Your love
and bear infirmity and tribulation.

Blessed be those who endure in peace
for by You most High they shall be comforted.

Praised be you my Lord, through Sister Death
From whom no living man can escape . . .

Praise and bless my Lord,
and give him thanks
and serve him with great humility.[16]

Reading this poem could become a daily meditation, in which we deliberately call to mind elements of the natural world that we can easily take for granted: the air, on which we depend for every second of our lives; the humility of water; or the playful vigour of fire. Finally, it reminds us of our own mortality, which we share with all of nature.

Poets too help us to recognise the holiness or 'otherness' of nature. Gerard Manley Hopkins (1844–89) captures the teeming vitality of spring which is almost an assault on our senses:

When weeds, in wheels, shoot long and lovely
and lush;
Thrush's eggs look little low heavens, and thrush
Through the echoing timber does so rinse and
wring
The ear, it strikes like lightnings to hear him sing;
The glassy peartree leaves and blooms, they brush
The descending blue; that blue is all in a rush
With richness; the racing lambs too
have fair their fling.[17]

Each bird, insect and stone wordlessly proclaims its unique existence:

As kingfishers catch fire, dragonflies draw flame;
As tumbled over rim in roundy wells
Stones ring; like each tucked string tells, each
hung bell's
Bow swung finds tongue to fling out broad its
name;
Each mortal thing does one thing and the same:
Deals out that being indoors each one dwells;
Selves – goes itself; myself it speaks and spells;
Crying *What I do is me: for that I came.*[18]

A contemporary poet, Mary Oliver (1935–2019), makes us consider the holiness of trees. Unlike human beings who are egotistically preoccupied with their future and what we call 'the meaning of life', they have their own, perhaps deeper wisdom:

Some will perish to become houses or barns,
fences and bridges.
Others will endure past the counting of years
And none will ever speak a single word of
complaint, as though language, after all,
did not work well enough, was only an early stage.
Neither do they ever have any questions to the
gods – which one is the real one, and what is
the plan.
As though they have been told everything
already and are content.[19]

Eager to find a living core at what appears to be lifeless, Oliver cannot bear to think that such a perfect being as a tree might not be sentient:

Is a tree as it rises delighted with its many
branches,
each one like a poem?

Are the clouds glad to unburden their bundles
of rain?

Most of the world says no, no, it's not possible.

I refuse to think to such a conclusion.
Too terrible it would be, to be wrong.[20]

Nature has its own perspective and wisdom that we can neither access nor wholly understand. It transcends us and remains something other, something holy. And as Job discovered and the Qur'an insists, we cannot know the reality we call 'God' without a reverent attention to the 'signs' of nature.

The Way Forward

The Qur'an reminds us of an important truth: the natural order cannot be sustained without balance. Our lack of respect for this delicate equilibrium has perhaps irreparably damaged our environment. The Qur'an insists this balance must also be evident in society and here too we fall short. Our religious scriptures and political traditions nearly all emphasise the importance of sharing essential resources equitably, yet despite our proud talk of democracy and justice, we have consistently failed to achieve this.

The ethos of the monotheistic religions, in particular, was shaped by prophets who raged against the injustices of their time. In the eighth century BCE, the Israelite prophet Amos virulently castigated the rulers of the day for their crimes. They had persecuted their countrymen, disembowelled pregnant women in an expansionist war and shown no concern for the poor:

> because they have sold the virtuous man for
> silver
> and the poor man for a pair of sandals,
> because they trample on the heads of ordinary
> people
> and push the poor out of their path.[21]

Amos was appalled by the inequity of Israelite society, where the poor starved while the aristocracy sprawled themselves over ivory couches, dining on expensive meat and drinking wine by the bowlful.[22] The Book of Isaiah opens with the oracles of a prophet inveighing against the punctilious ritual worship of the rich and powerful, when their hands are covered in blood:

> Take your wrongdoing out of my sight.
> Cease to do evil
> Learn to do good,

search for justice,
help the oppressed,
be just to the orphan,
plead for the widow.[23]

Jesus also spoke like an Israelite prophet. Luke's version of the Sermon on the Mount is more radical than Matthew's. The people who are blessed or 'happy' were not simply those who were 'poor in spirit' but those who were ostracised and oppressed by an unjust society:

Happy are you when people hate you, drive
 you out, abuse you, denounce your name as
 criminal on account of the Son of Man.
 Rejoice when that day comes and dance for
 joy, for then your reward will be great in
 heaven.
This was the way their ancestors treated the
 prophets.
But alas for you who are rich: you are having
 your consolation now.
Alas for you who have your fill now: you shall
 go hungry.
Alas for you who laugh now: you shall mourn
 and weep.

> Alas for you when the world speaks well of you! This was the way that their ancestors treated the false prophets.[24]

We would do well to remember this radical voice today.

In the modern world we rarely express the gratitude that our ancestors felt for the natural rhythms of nature. The ancient Egyptians did not take the natural order as a given but celebrated it as divine every day. For them the rising and setting of the sun was a sacred occurrence. Every morning Ra, the Sun Disc, rose from the darkness, and his course from east to west was observed by the Egyptian priests. Sunrise could never be taken for granted, for the journey of Ra and his entourage was fraught with peril. Every evening at sunset, he entered the world of darkness – the world of the dead ruled by Osiris. He therefore died every night to be reborn from the sky goddess the following morning, when the sacred journey began again. Similarly, the Egyptians believed that the annual flooding of the Nile, on which their agriculture depended, was a miraculous occurrence that repeated the moment the divine mound, the core of the world, rose from the primeval waters. Every summer, the low-lying fields and marshes returned to those abysmal waters but each time – miraculously, it seemed – the fields emerged transformed and fertile. Thus the Nile, like the sun, was divine. Nature was a series of miracles, which had to be celebrated.

Today, of course, we understand the science of the sunrise and no longer give it a second thought. But even if we don't regard these natural occurrences as the work of gods, maybe we should learn to marvel anew at the intricate rhythms of nature on which our daily lives depend. Perhaps we can find a particular poem or text and recite it once a day to express our gratitude to nature. After all, given the fragility of the planet, we can no longer take it for granted.

8

The Golden Rule

The Golden Rule – do not do to others what you would not have done to you – was developed independently by all the great religious traditions. It seems deeply rooted in human morality. It requires us to look into our hearts, identify what causes us pain and then refuse to inflict that on anybody else. What's more, this benevolence cannot be confined to your own congenial group; it has to be applied to everybody without exception. Compassion is the essence of religion and morality – and it is essential to the survival of humanity. That we constantly fail to put it effectively into practice is perhaps not surprising, as it runs counter to our ingrained selfishness, insisting that we dethrone ourselves from the centre of our world. It requires us to regard others as equal to ourselves, refuse to put ourselves into a privileged category, and deem the needs, desires and ambitions of our fellow human beings to be as valuable as our own.

One of the first to enunciate the Golden Rule was Confucius, for whom it was the essence of what he called *ren*,[1] a term that he refused to define because it did not fit any of the categories of the day. Ren could be summed up in two words, one of his disciples explained: *zhong* ('dutifulness'), fulfilling one's obligations to others; and *shu* ('consideration'), the ability to put oneself imaginatively in the place of another person and then act accordingly.[2] Thus 'shu' could also be translated as 'likening to oneself'.

When asked how ren could be applied to political life, Confucius replied:

> When in public comport yourself as if you were receiving an important guest, and in your management of the common people (min), behave as if you were overseeing a great sacrifice. Do not impose on others what you yourself do not desire.[3]

If a prince behaved towards other rulers in this way, there would be no more brutal wars. Conflict and hatred would melt away. Although Confucius refused to explain what ren was, he could still tell his disciples how to acquire it. You must use your own feelings as a guide to your treatment of others, he explained:

> As for ren, you yourself desire rank and standing; then help others to get rank and standing. You want to turn your merits to account; then help others to turn theirs to account – in fact, the ability to take one's own feelings as a guide – that is the sort of thing that lies in the direction of ren.[4]

If put continuously into practice – not just when we felt like it but 'all day and every day'[5] – Confucius believed ren would change the world far more effectively than a boost to the economy or victory in war.

Confucius insisted that it was pointless simply to focus on the development of interior attitudes of goodwill and courtesy, because physical behaviour could moderate internal feelings. That was why Confucians emphasised the importance of *li* ('ritual'). The Chinese understood that ritualised gestures of respect can teach us more deeply than rational lessons to honour the dignity of others. And our behaviour can change their conduct. We know that when we are treated with respect, we feel fundamentally, if only momentarily, enriched. In the same way, Confucius believed, the bodily gestures of li transformed those who received as well as those who performed them. Our public demeanour these days is determinedly casual, and it has many advantages. It makes us feel more at ease; we certainly don't wish to return to the stifling formal manners of the Victorian period. But if we attended to some traditional social conventions we might discover that we begin to internalise habits of courtesy and respect: opening the door for somebody; standing up when somebody comes into the room; shaking hands, smiling and making eye contact; offering up your seat on the bus. All these small rituals can create new habits of mind and heart.

For Confucians, ren, therefore, was a 'virtue' in the original sense of the word – a power (Latin: *virtus*) that emanates from a person and affects everyone around her. The virtues that Confucius emphasised – mutuality in human relations (*shu*), loyalty (*zhang*) and trust (*xin*) – all focused on one's behaviour towards others. Confucians were not working to edify their 'souls'; instead, they employed these virtues to develop a fulfilling daily practice and wider social ecosystem based on respect.[6]

Confucians believed that we are born only with the raw stuff of humanity – like an uncarved block of stone – and that to become a person of perfect humanity (with ren), our egotistic impulses have to be relinquished, 'all day and every day'.

Confucius reminds us of the importance of human dignity – that every person, whatever her rank, race or creed, is worthy of respect. In honouring the other we learn to lay aside the ego that is constantly clamouring for attention and pre-eminence. And external habits of respect help us to cultivate these virtues internally. As Hamlet instructs his erring mother: 'Assume a virtue if you have it not.'[7] When they become habitual, physical rites gradually create inner habits of reverence. Perhaps we in the West need to create rituals of our own to help us honour the stranger and the foreigner, the homeless and the destitute.

Confucius's original teaching focused on social life, but over the centuries, Confucians have extended it to the qi that nourishes the universe. By systematically putting the grasping and petty demands of the self aside, they were able to develop a new insight into the sacred forces that animate the natural world. Concern for the natural environment follows naturally from respect and reverence for humanity.

Mencius called this experience *hao ran zhi qi* ('flood-like qi'): 'Nourish it with integrity and place no obstacle in its path, and it will fill the space between Heaven-and-earth.'[8] The more you become aware of the sanctity of your fellow human beings, Mencius taught, the easier it becomes to perceive the sanctity of other beings and then love them too. You begin to understand that this holiness is also present in all the *wu* ('things') of nature.

> All the ten-thousand things (wanwu) are there in me. There is no greater joy for me than to find on self-examination that I am true to myself. Try your best to treat others as you would wish to be treated yourself, and you will find that this is the shortest way to benevolence (*ren*).[9]

Thus in Confucianism reverence for humanity and the natural world were inextricably combined.

During the ninth century BCE, Confucians responded to the challenge of Chinese Buddhism by incorporating Buddhist insights into their own classical texts. This movement, known as neo-Confucianism, not only made the compassionate ethos of Confucius and Mencius more radical, but also created an inspiring new theology of nature. The Confucian scholar Han Yu (768–824) drew people's attention to two obscure chapters in the ancient *Lijing* ('Classic of Rites'). The first was a short text known as the Great Learning (*Daxue*), which some attributed to Confucius's grandson Zisi (*c.* 483–404 BCE) and others to his disciple Zengzi. It insisted that scholarship was inseparable from spiritual development and social concern: 'The Way of the great learning lies in illuminating luminous virtue by treating the people with affection, and resting in perfect goodness (*ren*).'[10] The sage must 'extend his knowledge' through *gewu*, the 'investigation of things' – that is, of the wanwu of nature. A healthy family life, good government and a sound understanding of worldly affairs are rooted in a profound appreciation of nature because the natural world is our home and it affects everything we think and do. Today, we too must realise that our current efforts to devise effective policies to save our planet will fail, unless our priorities are right and our knowledge, our government and our spirituality are all firmly grounded in nature.

The second text recommended by Han Yu was the *Zhongyong* ('Doctrine of the Mean'), which was also attributed to Zisi.[11] The two elements of its name – *zhong* ('equilibrium') and *yong* ('normality') – indicate that society depends upon balance and moderation. But the text also calls for *cheng* ('sincerity'), which requires that human beings align their behaviour with the natural rhythms of the universe. We are not lords of the world, the *Zhongyong* tells us; we share the universe with the wanwu and must live in harmony with them, as Confucius had done:

> He conformed with the natural order governing the revolution of the seasons in heaven above, and followed the principles governing land and water below. He may be compared to earth in its supporting and containing all things, and to heaven in its overshadowing and embracing all things. He may be compared to the four seasons in their succession and to the sun and moon in their alternate shining. All things (*wu*) are produced and developed without injuring one another.[12]

It is essential that human society conforms to the rhythms of nature, which, unlike human affairs, proceed without harming others. Only if human beings form a deep partnership, a trinity, with heaven and earth,[13] and treat all the 'myriad things' as we would wish to be treated ourselves, will we become ren.[14]

We depend on the 'myriad things' for our very existence, so by serving, honouring and protecting them we participate actively in the creative processes of the cosmos and help to reconstitute the world.[15] Confucians had always emphasised the importance of filiality, but the *Zhongyong* maintains that human beings must also become sons and daughters of the universe.

We don't need to look for supernatural revelation. We simply need to recognise the sacrality of everything around us and observe how the myriad things tirelessly support one another:

> The heaven now before us is only this bright, shining mass; but when viewed in its unlimited extent, the sun, moon, stars, and constellations are suspended in it and all things are covered by it. The earth before us is but a handful of soil; but in its breadth and depth, it sustains mountains like Hua and Yüeh without feeling their weight, contains the rivers and seas without letting them leak away, and sustains all things. The mountain before us is only a fistful of straw; but in all the vastness of its size, grass and trees grow upon it, birds and beasts dwell upon it, and stores of precious things are discovered in it. The water before us is but a

> spoonful of liquid, but in all its unfathomable depth, the monsters, dragons, fishes and turtles are produced in them, and wealth become abundant because of it.[16]

Contemplating the endless generosity of the cosmos in this way is itself a transcendent experience: we can only exclaim, 'Ah! How beautiful and unceasing (*wumu buyi*)!'[17]

Instead of looking up to a distant heaven or deity to give his life meaning, the sage marvels at ordinary (*yong*) things on earth – a spoonful of water or a handful of soil. Did not Confucius, after all, achieve sagehood by focusing on what is 'near at hand' in both nature and humanity?[18] Sagehood was traditionally considered possible only for kings and noblemen but the *Zhongyong* insists that it is also attainable for 'men and women of simple intelligence'.[19] It merely requires practice and perseverance. So 'study it . . . and practise it earnestly', the *Zhongyong* tells us, and, above all, 'do not give up'.

In the eleventh century, China was repeatedly invaded by its neighbours and there was urgent need for reform. While most argued for a change in government or the military, a small group of neo-Confucians pioneered a spiritual revolution, by applying neo-Confucianism to political and social life, which they believed could not succeed unless they were in harmony with the sacred principle of the cosmos. Zhou Dunyi (1017–73) cultivated such a strong awareness of the sacred principle of life that he refused to cut the grass that grew beneath his window, because, he explained, 'the feelings of the grass' and his own were 'the same'.[20] This was not a mystical experience but an ethic derived from a habit of compassion, because instead of focusing exclusively on himself, Zhou deliberately tried to see things from the perspective of all people and all beings without exception. He developed such a strong conviction of his moral responsibility for all things that he was able to 'feel with' them as equals instead of focusing perpetually and egotistically on oneself. This ability, he explained, puts you on the road to sagehood because it 'makes one impartial and all-embracing'.[21] Yet the neo-Confucians never claimed to be sages. If you think you are a sage, they believed, it's a pretty sure sign that you aren't one![22]

For Zhang Zai (1020–77) all things had a moral nature of sorts, so the person who had deliberately cultivated a sense of the oneness of being could 'enter into' them:

> By enlarging one's mind, one can enter into all the things in the world. As long as anything is not yet entered into, there is still something outside his mind. The mind of ordinary people is limited to the narrowness of what is seen and what is heard. The sage, however, fully develops his nature . . . He regards everything in the world as his own self.[23]

Every 'thing' shared the essential ren that pervaded the cosmos. But humans had the capacity to realise the moral responsibilities of this relationship. Zhang expressed this beautifully in the 'Western Inscription' ('*Ximing*'), so called because it was inscribed on the western wall of his study. It begins: 'Heaven is my father and earth is my mother, and even such a small creature as I finds an intimate place in their midst.' In this one sentence, he epitomised the neo-Confucian vision. The inscription continues:

> Therefore, that which extends throughout all the universe I regard as my body and that which directs the universe I consider my nature.
>
> All people are my brothers and sisters and all things are my companions . . .

> One who disobeys the principle of Heaven violates virtue. One who destroys humanity is a robber. One who promotes evil lacks moral capacity. But one who puts his moral nature into practice and brings his physical existence to complete fulfilment can match Heaven and Earth.[24]

The 'Western Inscription' recalls Zhou Dunyi's reluctance to cut the grass; it positions suffering firmly in the neo-Confucian agenda. Zhang Zai once remarked that when he heard the cry of a donkey, he felt the same distress as the animal.[25]

Zhang's nephews, the Cheng brothers, transformed this piety into a movement. They were convinced that the 'Western Inscription' expressed lost teachings of Confucius.[26] For Cheng Hao (1032–85) understanding the 'oneness of things' was essential to the practice of ren, which in turn made a person one with nature. Again, this was not a mystical insight; it was achieved by the moral discipline of the Golden Rule: 'The man of *ren* takes Heaven-and-earth as being one with himself; to him there is nothing that is not himself. Having recognized them as himself what can he not do for them?'[27] Cheng Yi (1033–1107) taught his students to empty their minds of selfishness and cultivate reverence by means of gewu – the deep study of the 'principle of Heaven' that exists at the heart of all things. 'Every blade of grass and every tree,' Cheng Yi insisted, 'possesses a principle and should be examined.'[28]

Cheng Hao explained that if we form 'one body' with all other beings, we feel their suffering as our own: 'Not to feel disinterested sympathy with others is to lose the consciousness that they are one substance with myself.'[29] Before uttering a single word or performing a seemingly insignificant action, we must consider how it might affect others, including the 'myriad things' which, as the 'Western Inscription' pointed out, are not lifeless objects but our companions. This would take time and effort, the Cheng brothers told their students, but if they persevered they would eventually experience a joyful sense of liberation from the anxieties that beset the self-centred. They would acquire poise and serenity and find that they could be moral without becoming pompous and self-righteous.

This outlook permeates the *Reflections on Things at Hand*, an anthology of early neo-Confucian teachings compiled by the great Confucian reformer Zhu Xi (1130–1200).[30] Here, instead of extravagant religious zeal, the tone is one of gentleness, balance and poise. We learn that Zhou Dunyi's mind was 'free and unobstructed like the breeze on a sunny day and the clear moon [at night]' because in all his activities he was in harmony with the fundamental principles of nature.[31] He was completely at ease: 'When most people thought that a matter was extremely difficult, the Master did it as naturally as the irresistible flow of water. Even when he was hurried or startled, he never showed any expression of disturbance.'[32] His generosity was based on a continuous transcendence of self: 'Whenever he saw any good deed, he felt as though it had issued from himself. He would not do to others what he did not wish others to do to him.'[33] All this was possible, because he had calmly relinquished egotism and 'had no mind of his own'.[34]

But having no mind of one's own was not a relinquishment of personal responsibility. The neo-Confucians were not hermits; like many Confucians, they were engaged in government and brought serenity to their administrative duties. Zhu Xi explained that by constantly seeing the 'myriad things' as like the self, one was 'in accord with all creation . . . extremely impartial, and to have no mind or feeling of one's own was simply to respond spontaneously to all things as they come'.[35] Zhou Dunyi's mind may have been 'free and unobstructed', but in his official capacity, he was 'careful and strict, and treated others like himself'.[36] The aim was not to retire from the world but to bring assiduously acquired clarity and the discipline of the Golden Rule to public life.

Zhu Xi's descriptions of the neo-Confucian scholars contrast sharply with the conduct of many of today's public figures. Zhang Zai and Cheng Hao cultivated a mentality that the great Confucian philosopher Xunzi had described centuries earlier as 'empty, unified and still'. A mind was 'empty', Xunzi had explained, if it was constantly open to new impressions and so ready to change if the need arose. A mind was 'unified' if it did not force the complexity of life into a coherent, self-serving system. It was 'still' if it did not indulge in 'dreams and noisy fantasies', nurturing 'plots and schemes' that hinder true understanding.[37] Having 'no mind of your own' did not mean having no opinions, but being open to other perspectives. We too in this global age must learn to put the 'self' – be it personal, national, religious, cultural or ethnic – and the opinions that support it quietly to one side. As Laozi pointed out so long ago:

The reason there is great affliction is that I
have a self.
If I had no self, what affliction would I have?
Therefore to one who honours the world as
his self
The world may be entrusted,
And to one who loves the world as one's self
The world may be consigned.[38]

The Way Forward

The neo-Confucians bring together many of the concepts we have discussed in this book in a unique synthesis. It is beautifully expressed in Zhang Zai's 'Western Inscription', which provides not merely a vision of personal practice but a clear call to wider action. In their concern for humanity and the natural world the neo-Confucians see the two as inseparable – something that we in the West fail to appreciate. Crucial too is their cultivation of reverence. In the West we rather glorify irreverence, regarding it as a courageous challenge to the establishment and a mark of individuality, but it can be pure egotism. For the neo-Confucians, reverence was a religious awe which, consciously developed, led to a deep sense of responsibility. All too often, when we realise what damage we have done to our environment, our response is fear – and fear can be paralysing, quelling any creative initiative to address the problem. We need to learn how to revere nature in a positive, life-affirming sense, which then sets us free to cherish our environment rather than exploit it.

Above all, perhaps, we should embrace the neo-Confucians' vision of humanity forming 'one body with all things'. Awe at the natural world and unity between humanity and nature are beautifully expressed in the image of human beings forming a trinity with heaven and earth. It was a vision based on empathy rather than power, partition and blame; and it is acquired by the neo-Confucian discipline of 'quiet sitting' (*jingzuo*). Unlike yoga – which has often been downgraded in the West from a rigorous system for destroying the ego to an aerobic exercise – it is a state of repose, where you sit comfortably, not necessarily in the yogic position, and open your mind and heart to the natural world, feel its sights and sounds, and develop a sense of universal compassion. Compassion, of course, is not pity – which implies a sense of superiority – but a 'feeling with' the other.

The Golden Rule, first enunciated by Confucius, also expresses the ethos of compassion that lies at the heart of rabbinic Judaism and the Christian gospels. Yet these days there is often more emphasis on doctrines and practices, many of which post-date the scriptures. How often do we hear Christians vehemently condemning practices that neither Jesus nor Paul would have heard of? In these righteous, contentious and acrimonious times, we should remind ourselves of these words of Jesus:

> I say this to you who are listening: Love your enemies, do good to those who hate you, bless those who curse you, pray for those why treat you badly. To the man who slaps you on one cheek, present the other cheek also; to the man who takes your cloak from you, do not refuse your tunic . . . Treat others as you would like them to treat you. If you love those who love you, what thanks can you expect? Even sinners love those who love them. And if you do good to those who do good to you, what thanks can you expect? For even sinners do that much . . . Instead, love your enemies and lend without any hope of return . . .

> Be compassionate, as your Father is compassionate. Do not judge, and you will not be judged yourselves; do not condemn, and you will not be condemned.[39]

In a censorious and unforgiving world, we need compassion – the ability to feel with all others, whether we like them or agree with them or not – more urgently than ever.

9

Ahimsa

Like the Golden Rule, *ahimsa* is crucial to both the spiritual and social life, especially in the Indian traditions. A literal translation of the word as 'harmlessness' makes it sound rather tame but it is a radical concept: it prohibits any kind of injury to others, however minimal that might be. Yoga enthusiasts in the West would probably be astonished to hear that in classical yoga an aspirant was not allowed even to sit in the yogic position until she had mastered a rigorous moral programme. She had to observe five precepts to make sure she had herself under strict control; she was forbidden to steal, lie, take intoxicants or engage in sexual intercourse, but most importantly, she had to abide by ahimsa. One must not even swat an insect or speak unkindly to others.

Ahimsa had long been central to Indian spirituality but nobody took it as seriously as the Jains. The founder of this religious tradition, Vardhamana Jnatraputra (*c.* 497–425 BCE), had been born into the Kshatriya class but at the age of thirty he abandoned the world and set out to achieve enlightenment. His spiritual journey took over twelve years; he underwent asceticism, exposing his body to extreme conditions, but did not achieve the liberation he sought until he had developed ahimsa.[1] At this point he became known as Mahavira ('Great Hero'). Each human being, he believed, had a *jiva* ('soul'), which was luminous, blissful and intelligent. But so did every single animal, plant and rock, and even water, fire and air, all of which had been brought to their present existence by the *karma* ('deeds') of their past lives. It followed that every creature shares the same basic nature and must be treated with the courtesy and respect that we would wish to receive ourselves.[2] Even a plant has some kind of awareness and if it lives correctly by practising ahimsa in its own way, it might become a sacred tree in its next life and then progress slowly up the scale until it achieves humanity. Plants, animals and human beings can achieve enlightenment (*moksha*) only if they do not harm their fellow creatures.

For Mahavira, spiritual liberation was the result of practising non-violence. It was this insight, rather than demanding yogic exercises, that enabled him to achieve enlightenment. He found that ahimsa fundamentally altered his humanity and that he could now perceive all levels of reality simultaneously as though he were a god. Indeed, Mahavira realised that a deva was simply a being that had achieved a state of mind that transcended normal consciousness and consisted of absolute fraternity with all things. This state transcended mundane logic and rational thought: all Mahavira could say to describe it was '*Neti . . . neti*' ('Not this . . . not this'). But it was not inaccessible. Mahavira insisted that anybody who followed his regimen would achieve this state of mind and become a Jina ('Conqueror'). Mahavira had been born into the warrior class, but he was offering an alternative vision of heroism that rejected violence in favour of a different kind of courage. By battling his own aggressive instincts the Jain would win as much glory through ahimsa as a warrior would on the battlefield: it required the same kind of valour, discipline, determination and even ruthlessness – but all directed against oneself and one's own failings.

Later Jains would develop an elaborate cosmology and metaphysics that perceived their *karma* or 'deeds' as a physical substance like a fine dust, which weighted down the soul and prevented it from soaring to the summit of the universe. But Mahavira and his first disciples were not concerned with such matters. The only spiritual virtue they prized was ahimsa, which was not achieved until a Jain had acquired a profound empathy with every single being:

> All breathing, existing, living, sentient creatures should not be slain, nor treated with violence, nor abused, nor tormented, nor driven away. This is the pure, unchangeable, eternal law, which the enlightened ones who know have proclaimed.[3]

Jains had to convince themselves emotionally and at a profound level of their unconscious minds that even a stone had a jiva and was capable of pain. They achieved this insight with a programme of asceticism in which their bodily actions reshaped their minds. They had to walk at all times with extreme caution, lest they accidentally squashed an insect or trampled a blade of grass. They had to lay down objects with consummate care and were forbidden to move around at night lest they inadvertently damaged some hapless creature. They could never pluck fruit from a tree but had to wait until it fell of its own accord. Ultimately, the ideal was to abstain from any activity at all, because the tiniest movement could cause pain and suffering.

At all times, Jains had to be aware of the life force that dwelled in everything, so they were forbidden to light fires, dig or plough, and could drink only filtered water. They could not have any possessions, because everything has its own sacred jiva, which is sovereign and free.[4] Twice a day, a Jain would stand before his teacher and repent of any distress he may have inflicted 'by treading on seeds, green plants, dew, beetles, mould, moist earth and cobwebs'. He concluded by asking for forgiveness: 'I ask pardon from all living creatures. May all creatures pardon me. May I have friendship with all creatures and enmity toward none.'[5] If they observed these rules carefully Jains would develop a self-control and compassion that would inevitably bring them to enlightenment. It was a life of empathy.

Jainism is one of the first religious schools in India to make the Golden Rule the essence of its teachings: 'Persons endowed with intelligence and purified selves, should always behave toward other beings after the manner of that behaviour which they like others to observe towards themselves.'[6] It also insisted that ahimsa 'towards all living beings in all respects and for all time' was the essence of spirituality.[7] Unlike Buddhism, Jainism has never become a world religion, but its insistence on kindness and non-violence has spread throughout the subcontinent and is now also embedded in Buddhism, Hinduism and Indian Islam. In the West, we seem sometimes to have forgotten that 'To do harm to others is to do harm to oneself . . . We corrupt ourselves as soon as we intend to corrupt others. We kill ourselves as soon as we intend to kill others.'[8]

This ethos also entered political life. Ashoka (r. *c.* 264–223 BCE), the Mauryan emperor of India, instituted a policy of military restraint and moral reform, expressed in extraordinary edicts that he inscribed on cliff faces and pillars throughout his empire, promising to refrain from military force whenever possible, preaching kindness to animals, and announcing the planting of banyan trees to 'give shade for men and beasts'. He replaced the royal sport of hunting with pilgrimages to Buddhist shrines,[9] and though he eventually became a Buddhist, Ashoka had clearly imbibed Jain teachings. Akbar, the third Muslim emperor of India

(r. 1556–1605), studied with a Jain monk for two years. It was an experience that clearly influenced his policies: he prohibited animal slaughter on Jain festival days; he passed laws protecting mice, oxen, leopards, horses, fish, serpents, sheep, monkeys, roosters, dogs and pigs; and he himself gave up eating meat and hunting.[10] Ahimsa assumes that the other is like oneself, and is an important step towards perceiving the sacredness of all life; and as we are beginning to realise belatedly, humanity's welfare is dependent upon all other life forms on the planet.[11]

The *Mahabharata*, India's great epic, took centuries to evolve, with each generation contributing its own insights from *c.* 400 BCE to *c.* 400 CE. It seems to have begun as a Kshatriya saga but was eventually completed by Brahmin priests. Its epic story reflects a world of violence in which the assassination of kings is taken for granted, extermination is routine, and the *dharma* – the duties traditionally incumbent upon each social class – is a dead letter. We read of hideous battles and gruesome massacres. The so-called heroes often lie blatantly while their opponents, denounced as villains, behave with nobility. At the end of the catastrophic war between the two parties, 1,660,020,000 Kshatriyas have died, leaving a mere handful of survivors on each side.

But towards the end of the epic, Yudishthira, the pious but tainted king, seeks instruction from his old tutor Bhishma, who is close to death. In a world destroyed by violence, selfishness and cruelty, Bhishma talks about the virtue of ahimsa, which had clearly become a crucial teaching in Hindu priestly circles:

> The one who, desiring the pleasure of the self,
> abstains from killing helpless animals with a
> stick
> will attain happiness.
>
> That person who indeed sees beings as like his
> own self
> who has cast aside the stick and
> whose anger is conquered
> prospers happily in the life to come.
>
> Even the gods are bewildered at the path
> of the one who seeks the surrender of
> possessiveness,
> who sees all beings
> with the being of oneself.
>
> From not holding to the other

as opposite from oneself
there is the essence of *dharma*;*
the other proceeds [as other] due to desire.

In rejecting and giving, in pleasure and pain,
in the pleasant and unpleasant
the person who sees all things as the self goes
to *samadhi*.†

When the other strides among the others
then the other strides in the other
Let them imitate them in the world of living
beings
By this skill, all *dharma* is taught.[12]

At the end of its epic story, the *Mahabharata* displays the inevitable result of 'othering' in a battlefield littered with over a million stinking, mutilated corpses. It tells us that we must surrender our destructive egotism and selfishness, and cultivate instead an

* *dharma*: the order and custom that make life and the universe possible and therefore to the behaviour that maintains this order.

† *samadhi*: a state of consciousness in which a person is so absorbed in meditation that she loses awareness of the physical, natural world.

attitude that 'sees all things as the self', in which nothing is uniquely 'mine'. And instead of putting others in a distinct category, we are asked to pull down the barriers that separate us from all other beings.

The Way Forward

The profound empathy of the Jains asks us to realise that the world we live in is in pain and to take note of the damage we inflict upon our own and other species. In the West, mindfulness has become a popular spiritual exercise but is usually geared towards our own well-being. Perhaps we should extend it to cultivate a Jain-like awareness of the pain we inflict daily both on other humans and on nature.

Living the full Jain life would no doubt be too intense for most of us but we could still endeavour to reflect upon our behaviour – treading with caution, laying down objects with care, noting if we spoil or discard things. We should contemplate the life force of each thing we encounter in the course of a day. What kind of existence does this tree or that insect enjoy? It will not have consciousness as we know it, but it is alive in a mysterious, fascinating way. We should extend the Golden Rule to include species other than our own, even those that are seemingly insignificant. Their silence should inspire us to use our imagination to enter their lives and break free of our ingrained solipsism. Jains use their imagination to make themselves aware of the sacrality, fragility and unique identity of everything they encounter. They force themselves – all day and every day – to regard each thing carefully and with respect.

There is a remarkable instance of this outlook in Laurence Sterne's classic novel *Tristram Shandy* (1759). The hero's uncle Toby was of such 'a peaceful, placid nature' that he quite literally could not hurt a fly:

> Go – says he, one day at dinner, to an overgrown one which had buzzed about his nose, and tormented him cruelly all dinner time, – and which after infinite attempts, he had caught at last, as it flew by him; – I'll not hurt thee, says my uncle Toby, rising from his chair, and going across the room, with the fly in his hand, – I'll not hurt a hair of thy head: – Go, says he, lifting up the sash and opening his hand as he spoke, to let it escape; – go, poor devil, get thee gone, why should I hurt thee? – This world surely is wide enough to hold both thee and me.

And, the hero comments, even though he was just a child at the time, the incident 'instantly set my whole frame into one vibration of most pleasurable sensation'. He adds that 'the lesson of universal good-will then taught and imprinted by my uncle Toby, has never since been worn out of my mind'.[13] Jains would certainly have understood and appreciated Uncle Toby's gesture. We can create such moments ourselves every day by observing our behaviour and considering the sacrality and vulnerability of all creatures.

10

Concentric Circles

Zhang Zai, the author of the 'Western Inscription', believed that every thing in nature had a unique moral capacity, and that the sage, who understood the essential unity of being, was able to 'enter into' it empathically and imaginatively. As we have seen, this was a mental attitude rather than a mystical insight, acquired by a conscious and continuous extension of sympathy to more and more of the 'myriad things'. In China, it was expressed in the imagery of concentric circles, which was said to have gone back to Yao and Shun, the first kings of the Great Plain, in the twenty-third century BCE. Transmitted orally for centuries, their idea was recorded in the fourth-century BCE *Shujing* ('Classic of Documents'), which was obligatory reading for Chinese literati until the early twentieth century CE.

The *Shujing* depicts Yao as a man of *de* ('virtue'): 'He was reverent, intelligent, accomplished, sincere and mild. He was sincerely respectful and capable of modesty.' But Yao's de was not simply a personal quality; it was also an effective force – a charisma that had a positive influence on his surroundings, spreading out, with a ripple effect, until it embraced the entire world. First, Yao cherished his own family, but then he reached out in affection to the neighbouring clans, and finally to more remote kingdoms:

> His light covered the four extremities of the empire and extended to Heaven above and the Earth below. He was able to make bright his great virtue (de) and bring affection to the nine branches of the family. When the nine branches of the family had become harmonious, he distinguished and honored the hundred clans. When the hundred clans had become illustrious, he harmonized the myriad states. The numerous people were amply nourished and prosperous and became harmonious.[1]

At a time when our own thinking is becoming increasingly isolationist, focusing intensively on our own family, nation or culture, it is important to remember that from very early in their history the Chinese were deliberately thinking globally and their rituals of family life were carefully designed.

In the dynamic of concentric circles, the extension of each circle signifies a moment when we are compelled to transcend ourselves and our obsession with 'me' and 'mine'. The Chinese rituals of family life were carefully designed to make this expansion of sympathy habitual. First they were taught to revere their parents and siblings. Then, as they matured and grew older, they were taught to reach out from the family to the local community, learning to relinquish an ingrained nepotism. Next, they had to overcome parochialism and learn to serve the entire state. Finally, their patriotism had to be surmounted as they reached out in sympathy to the whole of humanity.

But to that we should add a new circle, which transcends our focus on humanity. When finally we realise that our very existence depends upon nature, it will be time to surrender our anthropocentrism and include the entire cosmos in our ultimate concern. 'You seek to establish yourself,' said Confucius, 'then seek to establish others.' Today these 'others' must include all the 'myriad things'.

By the tenth century CE, of course, the Chinese were already aware of this. The 'Great Learning', a chapter from the ancient 'Classic of Rites' that we considered earlier, prepared a *junzi*, step by step, for his social and political responsibilities. Unlike the Buddhists, who believed that one must achieve enlightenment before undertaking political action, the neo-Confucians insisted that political engagement was essential to our spiritual development. Here too the author sees this extension of sympathy in a series of concentric circles; but this time he begins with a *junzi*'s political responsibilities which required a psychological programme of self-cultivation that was rooted in a study of the 'things' of nature:

> Those in antiquity who wished to illuminate luminous virtue throughout the world would first govern their states; wishing to govern their states, they would first bring order to their families; wishing to bring order to their families, they would first cultivate their own persons; wishing to rectify their minds, they would first make their thoughts sincere (*cheng*); wishing to make their thoughts sincere, they would first

> extend their knowledge. The extension of knowledge lies in the investigation of things (*gewu*).

We need to be very clear about what the Chinese meant when they spoke about the 'things' (wu) of nature, because the word 'thing' has a very different meaning for us. The Oxford English Dictionary defines a 'thing' as 'a being without life or consciousness; an inanimate object'; and as 'a term which is now applied to a living person only in contempt, reproach or pity'. But we have seen that for the Chinese, the word wu had very different connotations. Cheng Yi told his pupils to look deeply into every 'thing' around them, because each one had a 'principle', a sacred quality or essence which made even the humblest object precious and significant. It was this awareness that made Zhou Dunyi so reluctant to cut the grass outside his window and why, in the 'Western Inscription', Zhang Zai also made it clear that the wanwu were not lifeless objects but must be treated as friends and equals.

This does not mean, of course, that we should anthropomorphise the 'things' of nature, endowing them with human qualities. Each sacred principle is unique; each 'thing' has its own mode of existence and consciousness which is entirely different from our own and must be respected for what it is. This carefully cultivated concern and respect for every 'thing' in nature lay at the heart of Jain spirituality too and it also inspired Uncle Toby's anxiety for the fly. It is our modern failure to foster a reverence for these 'things' that has resulted in our serious environmental crisis. So, if we want to save our planet, we too must cultivate this ancient conviction that every natural thing is inseparable from our ultimate concern. We humans have the capacity to appreciate consciously, deliberately and imaginatively the underlying unity of things, which the 'Great Learning' illustrates with the image of a tree, whose branches reach out to the all-embracing sky but which is rooted deeply in the earth, meaning that knowledge of the wider world and good government must be grounded in the natural world.

In another passage the concentric circles move outwards again, from the wu of nature, to the mind of the individual, to his or her family and finally to the whole world:

> It is only when things (*wu*) are investigated that knowledge is extended; when knowledge is extended, that thoughts become sincere; when thoughts become sincere that the mind is rectified; when the mind is rectified that the

> person is cultivated; when the person is cultivated that order is brought to the family; when order is brought to the family that the state is well governed; when the state is well governed that peace is brought to the world.

The 'Great Learning' ends with an appeal to the individual: we cannot simply leave the fate of the world in the hands of our political leaders; every single one of us has responsibility. We must all order our priorities, each one of us contributing in whatever way we can to ensure the peace and integrity of the world within our immediate communities and ecosystems, and internationally, before it is too late:

> From the Son of Heaven to ordinary people, all, without exception should regard cultivating the person as the root. It can never happen that the root is disordered and the branches are ordered. It should never be that what is significant is regarded lightly and what is insignificant is regarded with gravity. This is called knowing the root; this is called the perfection of knowledge.

The passing of each concentric circle signifies a moment in which yet another barrier between ourselves and others is transcended. It is not a process that is carried out once and completed; rather it represents a continuous dynamic that encourages us to reach out beyond ourselves. It is badly needed today, when despite the fact that we live more closely entwined than ever before, we remain dangerously estranged. The present surge of nationalism around the world reveals an impulse towards self-isolation which, as the Covid pandemic has made abundantly clear, is impossible.

The Chinese concept of the concentric circles represents just one approach to the enlightenment and self-transcendence that we need to overcome our predicament. The Buddha provides us with another. He is often depicted sitting with his eyes closed in the yogic position, seemingly immersed in the depths of his own being; but, in fact, the contemplative effort that enabled him to achieve enlightenment was based on the transcendence of self and selfishness that was relentlessly expansive and outward-looking. He believed that this novel form of contemplation would create a new kind of human being, which was no longer dominated by greed and egotism. Compassion now took the place of self-punitive asceticism. Traditionally, a yogin had learned to achieve a higher state of consciousness by cultivating four successive *jhānas* ('stages') of tranced concentration, each of which yielded greater spiritual insight. But when the Buddha made his bid for enlightenment, he fused each jhāna with states that he called the 'immeasurables' (*appamana*). Every day, he deliberately evoked the emotion of love – 'that huge, expansive and immeasurable feeling that knows no hatred' – and directed it to one of the four corners of the world. There was nothing selective about this love: not a single living plant, animal, demon, friend or enemy was omitted from this zone of benevolence.

In the first jhāna, the Buddha cultivated a feeling of affection for everybody and everything. This was not easy. Most of us have deeply ingrained likes and dislikes; we approve of some things and condemn others. But these preferences often reflect aspects of our egotism and self-regard. We get a buzz of righteousness by denouncing certain people and things. We have to remind ourselves how little we know of them and how, if we had experienced life differently, we might have an entirely different perception. When the Buddha mastered this first jhāna, he progressed to the second, learning to suffer with other people and things through empathy – just as he had felt the suffering of the grass and insects in the ploughed field as a boy. Again, there could be nothing selective about this compassion: it was not enough simply to empathise with people or things that were natural to him. The Buddha had to feel with the pain of all others without exception, even people or 'things' he disliked. In the third jhāna, he cultivated a 'sympathetic joy' and rejoiced at the happiness of others without reflecting on how this might rebound upon himself.

When the Buddha finally reached the fourth jhāna, he was so deeply immersed in the happiness and suffering of others that he had acquired total equanimity, feeling neither attraction nor antipathy. This was an extremely difficult state to reach and maintain, since it required the yogin to divest himself of our deeply instinctive egotism that mechanically looks to see how other things or people might benefit or discommode oneself.[2] The Buddha had to abandon all personal interest in favour of benevolence. Where traditional yoga at that time had built up in the yogin a state of impervious autonomy, the Buddha was learning to transcend himself in an act of love towards all other beings.

The immeasurables were designed to pull down the barricades we erect between ourselves and others in order to protect our fragile ego. As the Buddha's mind gradually broke free of its customary caution and self-concern, it became 'expansive, without limits, enhanced, without hatred or petty malevolence'.[3] But such a strict regime was not for everybody; indeed, not many yoga practitioners in the West today either desire or are capable of such radical elimination of egotism. The Buddha was well aware of this. He once preached a sermon to the Kalamans, a people who lived on the northernmost fringe of the Ganges Basin and who were confused by the complexity of some of the new teachings. The Buddha introduced them to a meditative technique through which a lay person could practise a version of the immeasurables. First, the Kalamans were to empty their minds of ill will and envy and then, once these negative states were in abeyance, direct feelings of loving kindness in all four directions. As they did so, imbued with 'abundant, exalted, measureless loving kindness', they would break through the barriers that confined them to a limited, self-bound worldview and – even if just for a moment – experience an ekstasis that took them out of themselves, and 'above, below, around and everywhere'. They would feel their hearts expand.[4] This state is well illustrated in a poem from the Pali Canon:

> Let all beings be happy! Weak or strong, of
> high, middle or low estate,

small or great, visible or invisible, near or far
away,
alive or still to be born – may they all be
perfectly happy!

Let nobody lie to anybody or despise any
single being anywhere.
May nobody wish harm to any single creature,
out of anger or hatred!

Let us cherish all creatures, as a mother her
only child!
May our loving thoughts fill the whole world,
above, below, across – without limit; a
boundless goodwill toward the whole world,
Unrestricted, free of hatred and enmity.[5]

This simple prayer – not directed to any saint or deity – may be recited and meditated upon daily, helping us to build up gradually the generous outreach that we have considered in this chapter.

The Way Forward

We urgently need to cultivate an empathy with our fellow human beings that transcends national, political, racial and other ideological boundaries, as well as a sense of responsibility – and love – towards the 'myriad things' of nature. Notice that the Buddha's prayer is for 'all creatures' – visible or invisible, alive or still to be born, human or natural. What is required is unrestricted goodwill. This cannot be just a vague, pious wish. The Covid pandemic has demonstrated the power of nature and our own vulnerability; it has also shown how interconnected we are. Before the pandemic, there was a surge of new environmental concern across the world. Yet as we are desperate to return to normality after lockdown we are determined to recover lost freedom and dream again of holidays in distant resorts. Can we afford these liberties? Can we simply board aeroplanes with the same panache as ever, knowing how air travel damages the atmosphere? These are questions that we must consider globally, with our neighbours in all parts of the world, if we want to save the planet.

The Confucian scholar Tu Weiming has suggested a new version of the concentric circles.[6] As in the 'Great Learning', we start by working on the self. We might say that we do too much of that these days; we are perhaps too focused on our own health and wellbeing, our personal progress. But this step involves a re-examination of what Tu calls the dark side of the Enlightenment mentality that is present to some degree in all of us, fuelled by the desire not only to know, but also to conquer and subdue. Most of us are not in a position to do this politically, but we should make ourselves aware of our interactions with family members, colleagues, friends and rivals whom we belittle in various ways in order to inflate ourselves. Next we reach out compassionately to develop our sense of family, which must also include those members whom we dislike or who disapprove of us. Then we consider our community, and here, modern technology and communications can help us widen our community and transcend parochialism. The next circle encompasses society which must purge itself of the ethnocentricity that continues to surface in racist incidents such as the murder of George Floyd. We keep living in nation states but nationalism must be reformed and purged of the chauvinism that led to the world wars and has recently resurfaced around the world. Finally, we reach out to the cosmos that embraces us all and here we must seek to establish harmony between humanity and nature.

The great Chinese scholar and statesman Wang Yang-ming (1472–1529) in his commentary on the 'Great Learning' argued that human beings are not naturally anthropocentric. He pointed out that when a child hears the pitiful cries of animals about to be slaughtered, he finds their suffering difficult to bear, proving that his humanity 'forms one body' with other beings and things:

> When he sees plants broken and destroyed, he cannot help feeling pity. This shows that his humanity forms one body with plants . . . Yet even when he sees tiles and stones shattered and crushed, he cannot help a feeling of regret . . . This means that even the mind of a small man necessarily has the humanity that forms one body with all.[7]

But we do not merely share the same nature as animals, plants and other 'things'; as the *Zhongyong* tells us, humanity also forms a trinity with heaven and earth.

Tu Weiming argues that we must go beyond the secular humanism that formed the anthropocentric ethos of the Enlightenment. We should develop an anthropo*cosmic* mentality that unites the individual with the community and preserves the harmony between the human species and the non-human world. This underlying sense of nature's inherent sacrality relies on the dynamic vitalism of the qi, the substance of life, which others have called the Dao, the Brahman, God or the sacred. It lies at the heart of the ongoing creativity and renewal of nature, which we explored at the beginning of this book.

We should make the contemplation of Tu's concentric circles part of our daily routine, to be performed for fifteen or twenty minutes while walking the dog, travelling to work or even doing a humdrum task. The object is to extend the mind from what is 'near at hand', breaking down barriers of egotism and habits of self-regard, to realise our profound connection with and, indeed, our dependence upon all our fellow creatures and the natural world. In the process, we will develop new habits of mind and heart. We should start, perhaps, with nature, looking closely at our immediate environment, making ourselves aware of the magnificence of trees, flowers, birdsong and clouds, until they are no longer just a backdrop to our lives but a daily marvel. We must also recognise the essential 'holiness' or 'otherness' in nature that makes it more than a resource; we should recall what sages have said about its mystery and inscrutability. We should not leave this circle, therefore, until we can feel our minds stretching, like Job's, or until, like him, we put our hand to our mouth in recognition of the limitations of our knowledge.

When we move on to embrace the circles that contain our fellow human beings, we must extend our compassion, our ability to 'feel with', even to those who we do not know or understand. In acknowledging our differences we should note that any single worldview is inadequate and repent our apathy towards people who do not share our ethnicity, class, sex, nationality, politics or religious beliefs.

We should conclude with a thoughtful recitation of the Buddha's prayer, 'Let all beings be happy', noting that it is not addressed to a deity but to ourselves: it is asking us to extend our compassion and sympathy to all others without exception. We should mark the emphatic inclusivity of the prayer and its refusal to accept boundaries of any kind: empathy is 'without limit, a boundless good will towards the whole world, unrestricted, free of hatred and enmity'. We should remember that the Buddha achieved enlightenment not by polishing his soul, but by directing expansive feelings of love to every being in the world. We may not reach Nirvana, but the spirit of this prayer is within our capacity and essential for the well-being of the world.

Epilogue

We began our exploration of sacred nature with Wordsworth's childhood vision, where every meadow, grove and stream seemed bathed in a 'celestial light', which faded when he reached adulthood. Yet in a later poem, he tells us that he had 'learned' to look at the natural world differently; by cultivating a contemplative mindset he had achieved a 'blessed mood', when

> . . . with an eye made quiet by the power
> Of harmony, and the deep power of joy,
> We see into the life of things.[1]

This 'blessed mood' is clearly similar to what Confucians and Daoists, Hindus and Buddhists, Greeks and Sufis, cultivated for centuries. We have seen that they too developed receptive states of mind – in yoga, quiet sitting, meditation, poetry and ritual – that enabled them to look beneath the surface of reality to discover the sacrality immanent in the 'things' of nature.

As we approach the end of this book, it seems fitting to come full circle and see how Wordsworth's friend and fellow poet Samuel Taylor Coleridge (1772–1834) viewed the natural world, because he too has an important message for us. Coleridge knew that we need silence and a degree of solitude to appreciate the wonders of nature. Only then does it come to life and enter our consciousness deeply. In his poem 'Frost at Midnight', we find him sitting by the fireside keeping watch over his infant son. The house is quiet and tranquil; the poet is relaxed and, aware of the intense stillness of nature outside his cottage, lets his mind roam in a way not unlike the neo-Confucian practice of quiet sitting:

> The Frost performs its secret ministry
> Unhelped by any wind.[2]

He knows that frost is not simply a physical phenomenon – the result of a drop in temperature – and that, emerging mysteriously from apparent nothingness, it has a secret life of its own, intricate and complex like the spider's web that David Abram saw in a mountain cave that rainy night. Coleridge attributes a kind of life and purpose to the frost, different from our own, perhaps, but something we can relate to. In this way, the 'things' of nature become our companions. The silence, broken only by an owlet's cry, is so intense that it is almost distracting – it 'vexes meditation with its strange / And extreme stillness'.[3] Yet it ultimately enables him to think deeply.

So, to glimpse the sacrality of the natural world requires a degree of quiet and solitude that is hard to come by today. Indeed, we seem to find silence alien and often deliberately eliminate it from our lives. We wear earphones while exercising or walking in a park and chatter tirelessly on our mobile phones on a deserted beach. As a result, the sounds of nature have retreated and become increasingly distant from our minds and hearts. If we want to halt the environmental crisis, we need first, like Coleridge, to seek a silent receptiveness to the natural world, bringing it into our lives little by little every day. As he feels the 'hush of nature' harmonising with the stillness of his own mind, Coleridge promises his baby son that he will not grow up in towns and cities, as the poet himself did, but will 'wander like a breeze / By lakes and sandy shores'. Immersed in nature, he will see and hear:

The lovely shapes and sounds intelligible
Of that eternal language which thy God
Utters, who from eternity doth teach
Himself in all, and all things in himself.[4]

As a result of his attentiveness, Coleridge did not experience a deity confined to heaven, like the God of Newton or Descartes; instead, like nearly all the great poets, mystics and philosophers we have met in this book, he sees the divine as inseparable from nature. In an earlier poem, 'The Eolian Harp', he had asked his readers to cultivate a similar awareness for themselves:

O! the one Life within us and abroad,
Which meets all motion and becomes its soul,
A light in sound, a sound-like power in light,
Rhythm in all thought, and joyous everywhere.[5]

This vision of the 'one life' uniting the whole of reality recalls the Chinese concept of *qi*, the Indian notion of the Brahman, and Ibn al-Arabi's account of the divine sigh of sorrow at the heart of all being.

The 'one life' is also the driving force of Coleridge's most famous poem, 'The Rime of the Ancient Mariner', which has a stern message for us today. Although written in the style of a late-medieval ballad, its language deliberately archaic, it speaks directly to our current environmental crisis. Literary critics believe that the poem is set in the late Middle Ages when, as we have seen, theologians in Oxford, Bologna and Paris were beginning to devise a new theology that separated God and nature. The story begins at a wedding, where an elderly mariner, with a 'long grey beard and glittering eye',[6] seizes one of the guests and prevents him joining the celebrations. The Mariner relates the tragic, hypnotic story of his final voyage. At first, heading south in fair weather, his ship made good progress, but once it entered the Antarctic region, it was becalmed, stuck in a frightening, alien world of icebergs, mist and snowy cliffs. But suddenly an albatross, a large white bird with long slender wings, came flying through the fog and landed on the ship. Its dramatic arrival seemed a good omen, and the cheered sailors fed the bird and hailed it in God's name. With the albatross circling protectively overhead, the helmsman steered the ship through the ice and a good wind blew it into more clement weather.

But at this point in his story, the Mariner suddenly grows pale. 'God save thee, ancient Mariner,' cries the Wedding Guest, 'Why look'st thou so?' With startling brevity, the Mariner replies:

With my crossbow
 I shot the Albatross.[7]

The Mariner makes no excuse for this action; nor does he attempt to explain it. Yet we discover that there are terrible consequences for this spontaneous, senseless act, violating the sanctity of the 'one life' that we share with the natural world.

Like the Mariner, we have all committed crimes against nature that seem so trivial and unworthy of notice that we think nothing of them and would not dream of discussing them with others. It is not that we deliberately overlook activities that we know to be damaging; despite the ceaseless warnings of environmentalists, we simply do not see what we do as important. We feel no need either to excuse or to explain ourselves. We are still throwing away plastic, even though we know it ends up in the oceans and imperils marine life. We think nothing of driving our cars to the shops when we could easily walk or use public transport. We seem to regard flying as a human right, even though we know that it pollutes the atmosphere. Like the Mariner, we dismiss these activities from our mind, and rarely discuss their possible repercussions. The Mariner too would almost certainly have forgotten the albatross, killed on a passing whim, had the spirits of nature not stepped in.

At first, there were no repercussions for the crime. In fact, the weather improved and the sailors, who had initially been appalled by the heartless slaughter of the albatross, changed their minds and thus became complicit in the Mariner's sin.

> 'Twas right, said they, such birds to slay.
> That bring the fog and mist.[8]

But when the ship entered the Pacific Ocean, nature took its revenge: the ship was becalmed and lay idle under the blazing sun: 'every tongue, through utter drought, was withered at the root,'[9] the narrator tells us. Nature itself seemed repellent: 'Yea, slimy things did crawl with legs / Upon the slimy sea.'[10] The crew now blamed the Mariner for their plight and hung the albatross's corpse around his neck to replace the crucifix he had worn hitherto. Deprived of water, unable to speak, the sailors died one by one, gazing at the Mariner with hatred, their souls passing him, he recalled, 'like the whizz of my crossbow'.[11] Finally, he was left alone, appalled that:

The many men so beautiful
And they all dead did lie:
And a thousand, thousand slimy things
Lived on, and so did I.[12]

The Mariner feels only contempt for the natural world, regarding the human species alone as valuable – an attitude that perhaps underlies much of our own behaviour.

But it was the natural world that saved the Mariner. For seven days he lay beside his dead companions, unable to bear the curse that remained in their eyes. But one night, when he happened to turn his gaze upwards, he saw the moon rising in the sky. Hitherto, he had experienced the 'horned' or 'star-dogged' moon as a remote planet of little interest and with no real life of its own. But that suddenly changed:

The moving Moon went up the sky,
And nowhere did abide:
Softly she was going up
And a star or two beside.[13]

Coleridge's gloss beside this stanza is in fact more 'poetic' than the verse, as it describes the Mariner's sudden change of heart:

> In his loneliness and fixedness, he yearneth toward the journeying Moon, and the stars that still sojourn, yet still move onward; and every where the blue sky belongs to them, and this is their appointed rest, and their native country and their own natural homes, which they enter unannounced, as lords that are certainly expected, and yet there is a silent joy at their arrival.

The Mariner was feeling the affinity between his predicament and the journeying moon. A traveller himself, he suddenly has a yearning for homecoming, fellowship and the 'silent joy' of communion with others – *all* others, not simply other human beings. Instead of simply observing nature as inert, mechanical and separate from himself, his imagination endowed it with life and he felt a profound fellowship with the moon. When he turned his gaze back to the sea, he saw the water-snakes, which he had earlier dismissed as repellent 'slimy things', with new eyes:

> They moved in tracks of shining white,
> And when they reared, the elfish light
> Fell off in hoary flakes.
>
> Within the shadow of the ship

I watched with rich attire:
Blue, glossy green, and velvet black,
They coiled and swam; and every track
Was a flash of golden fire.

O happy living things! No tongue
Their beauty might declare:
A spring of love gushed from my heart,
And I blessed them unaware.[14]

It was a moment of ekstasis, a 'stepping outside' of ego and benumbing self-preoccupation. At once the spell snapped: the Mariner was able to pray and the albatross fell from his neck 'like lead into the sea'.[15]

In order to redeem the natural world, we too should learn to align ourselves with it emotionally and realise our affinity with and utter dependence upon it. We must make a deliberate effort to look beneath the surface of nature and experience sacrality for ourselves, as Kabbalists, Muslims, Christians, Confucians, Daoists and Hindus have for centuries. They managed this not by scientific study but through creativity and art – with rituals, poetry, music and bodily gestures that have a profound effect on mental life. We too must learn to see nature more intimately, and this requires imagination.

The Mariner's sudden vision was not a passing phase. On his homeward voyage, while listening to birdsong, he found that because of this hard-won, new-found insight, he was able to see the connection between heaven, earth and nature:

And now 'twas like all instruments,
Now like a lonely flute;
And now it is an angel's song
That makes the heavens be mute.

It ceased; yet still the sails made on
A pleasant noise till noon,
A noise like of a hidden brook
In the leafy month of June,
That in the sleeping woods all night
Singeth a quiet tune.[16]

But we cannot confine our love to the natural world; it must be extended to our fellow human beings. The Mariner learned this lesson too. He tells the Wedding Guest that though he will remain forever an outcast and outsider, he has one solace:

To walk together to the kirk
With a goodly company! –

To walk together to the kirk
And all together pray.[17]

Prayer cannot be a private union with a supernatural God; it must include our fellow humans and the 'things' of nature:

He prayeth well, who loveth well
Both man and bird and beast.

He prayeth best, who loveth best
All things both great and small;
For the dear God who loveth us
He made and loveth all.[18]

At the end of the poem the Wedding Guest, who, like ourselves, has had to absorb the deep significance of the Mariner's tale, has no heart for frivolous festivities any more and turns away from the bridegroom's door:

He went like one that hath been stunned,
And is of sense forlorn:
A sadder and a wiser man,
He rose the morrow morn.[19]

We too perhaps leave this book sadder and wiser, recognising the gravity of our environmental predicament and our personal responsibility for it, but also intent on a transformation of mind and heart that will impel us to repair the damage. We have seen how nature was revered by the great sages, mystics and prophets of the past. It is now up to us to revive that knowledge and commitment and recover our bond with the natural world.

Acknowledgements

This book is dedicated, with gratitude and love, to Felicity Bryan, my friend and agent for over thirty years, who quite simply changed my life. Without her I would never have become a writer. But it also bears the indelible stamp of Dan Frank, my American editor, who contributed his invaluable insights so generously until his untimely death. Both are irreplaceable.

But I owe, as always, an immense debt to my friend and editor Jörg Hensgen at the Bodley Head, whose enthusiasm, commitment and invaluable insights made the editing process a joy. My gratitude too to my editors Louise Dennys at Knopf Canada, Andrew Miller at Knopf in New York and Stuart Williams at the Bodley Head for their friendship and encouragement. At the Bodley Head I would like to thank copy-editor Samuel Wells, proofreader Katherine Fry, indexer Ben Murphy, jacket designer Matt Broughton and publicist Ryan Bowes for their skill and expertise in producing and promoting the book. And many thanks to my loyal agents: Catherine Clark, who has stepped so brilliantly into Felicity's shoes; my Canadian agent Anne McDermid; and, of course, Peter Ginsberg and Andrew Nurnberg, who have both looked after me with such loyalty and affection over the years. And thanks too to Michele Topham at Felicity Bryan Associates, for her unfailing kindness, patience and practical help.

Notes

Introduction

1 David Abram, *The Spell of the Sensuous: Perception and Language in a More-than-Human World* (New York, 1996), 7–10
2 Ibid., 19
3 Lucien Lévy-Bruhl, *How Natives Think*, trans. Lilian A. Clare (New York, 2015)
4 Genesis 1:28; unless otherwise stated, all quotations from the Bible are taken from *The Jerusalem Bible* (London, 1966)
5 Mircea Eliade, *The Myth of the Eternal Return: Or, Cosmos and History*, trans. Willard J. Trask (Princeton, NJ, 1966), 104
6 Thomas Aquinas, *Summa Theologiae* 8.1, in Timothy McDermott, trans. and ed., *Summa Theologiae: A Concise Translation* (London, 1989)
7 René Descartes, *Les Meteores*, in Paul J. Olscamp, trans. and ed., *Discourse on Method, Optics, Geometry and Meteorology* (Indianapolis, 1965), 203
8 Isaac Newton to Richard Bentley, 10 December 1691, in *The Correspondence of Isaac Newton*, Vol. 3, ed. H. W. Turnbull, 236

9 Ibid., 108

10 Samuel Clarke, 'A Discourse Concerning the Unchangeable Obligations of Natural Religions and the Truth and Certainty of Christian Religion', in Richard Watson, ed., *A Collection of Theological Tracts* (London, 1985), 246

11 Seyyed Hossein Nasr, 'The Spiritual and Religious Dimensions of the Environmental Crisis', in Barry McDonald, ed., *Seeing God Everywhere: Essays on Nature and the Sacred* (Bloomington, IN, 2003), 94–5

1. Mythos and Logos

1 Johannes Sloek, *Devotional Language*, trans. Henrik Mossin (Berlin and New York, 1996), 53–96

2 Ibid., 50–2, 68–71

3 Mark Johnson, *The Body in the Mind: The Bodily Basis of Meaning, Imagination and Reason* (Chicago, 1987)

4 Gavin Flood, *The Ascetic Self: Subjectivity, Memory and Tradition* (Cambridge, 2004), 218–25

2. Sacred Nature

1 Willard J. Peterson, 'Fang-chih: Western Learning and the Investigation of Things', in William Theodore de Bary, ed., *The Unfolding of Neo-Confucianism* (New York, 1975)

2 Tu Weiming, 'The Continuity of Being: Chinese Visions of Nature', in Tu Weiming, *Confucian Thought: Selfhood as Creative Transformation* (Albany, NY, 1985), 137–8

3 Trans. Harold D. Roth, *Original Tao: Inward Training and the Foundations of Taoist Mysticism* (New York, 1999), 46
4 Analects 15.23; trans. Edward Slingerland, *Confucius: Analects* (Indianapolis and Cambridge, 2004)
5 Mencius 7A.4; unless otherwise stated, quotations from Mencius are from D. C. Lau, trans., *Mencius* (London, 1970)
6 Daodejing (DDJ) 1. 1-2; unless otherwise stated, quotations from the Daodejing are from D. C. Lau, trans., Lao Tzu, *Tao Te Ching* (London, 1963)
7 DDJ 1.1–2
8 Toshihiko Izutsu, *Sufism and Taoism: A Comparative Study of Key Philosophical Concepts* (Berkeley, Los Angeles and London, 1983), 302–413
9 DDJ 40
10 Ibid. 62
11 Ibid. 42.93
12 Ibid. 52; in *Tao Te Ching*, trans. Stephen Aldiss and Stanley Lombardo (Indianapolis, 1992)
13 DDJ 40.88
14 Ibid. 16.85
15 Zhuangzi 19; in Burton Watson, ed. and trans., *The Complete Works of Zhuangzi* (New York, 2013), 147
16 Ibid. 6; in Watson, *Complete Works of Zhuangzi*, 47
17 Jan Gonda, *The Vision of the Vedic Poets* (New Delhi, 1984), 27–34, 56–7
18 Rig Veda (RV) 10.127.1; trans. William K. Mahony, *The Artful Universe: An Introduction to the Vedic Religious Imagination* (Albany, NY, 1998), 18–19

19 RV 10.68.1; trans. Wendy Doniger, *The Rig Veda: An Anthology* (London, 1981)
20 RV 1.124.7
21 Tatyana J. Elizarenkova, *Language and Style of the Vedic Rishis* (Albany, 1995), 17–18; Gonda, *Vision*, 89
22 Stephanie W. Jamison and Michael Witzel, 'Vedic Hinduism', in Arvind Sharma, ed., *The Study of Hinduism* (Columbia, SC, 1992), 67
23 Mahony, *Artful Universe*, 3–4, 46–50
24 Jan Gonda, *Four Studies in the Language of the Veda* ('s-Gravenhage, 1955), 129, 133
25 RV 2.13.17; 3.38.2–3; 3.61.7; 5.85.1–2, 5–6
26 Ibid. 3.88.2; trans. Mahony, *Artful Universe*
27 Bede Griffiths, *A New Vision of Reality: Western Science, Eastern Mysticism and Christian Faith,* ed. Felicity Edwards (London, 1992 edn), 58–9
28 Brhadaranyaka Upanishad 5.3.1; trans. Patrick Olivelle, *Upanishads* (Oxford, 1996)
29 Kaushitiki Upanishad 4.20; trans. Mahony, *Artful Universe*, 166
30 Brahmabindu Upanishad 12; trans. Mahony, *Artful Universe*, 164
31 Mahony, *Artful Universe*, 169
32 Arnand Sharma, 'Attitudes to Nature in the Early Upanishads', in Lance E. Nelson, ed., *Purifying the Earthly Body of God: Religion and Ecology in Hindu India* (Albany, NY, 1998)
33 Chandogya Upanishad 7. 1; trans. Sharma, 'Attitudes to Nature'
34 Ibid. 7.6; trans. Sharma, 'Attitudes to Nature'

35 Jean-Paul Sartre, *The Imaginary: A Phenomenological Psychology of the Imagination*, trans. Kenneth Williford and David Rudrauf (London, 2012)
36 Paul Williams, *Mahayana Buddhism: The Doctrinal Foundations* (London, 1989), 30–4, 72–81
37 Han Shan, *The Collected Songs of Cold Mountain* (Port Townsend, WA, 1983), 79
38 Charles Eliot, *Japanese Buddhism* (London, 1969), 160
39 Ibid., 67–8
40 Acts 17:34
41 Denys Turner, *Eros and Allegory: Medieval Exegesis of the Song of Songs* (Milton Keynes, 1995), 47–68; Denys Turner, *The Darkness of God: Negativity and the Sacred* (Cambridge, 1995), 2–47; Eric D. Perl, *Theophany: The Neoplatonic Philosophy of Dionysius the Areopagite* (New York, 2007)
42 *The Divine Names* (DN) 712, A–B; quotations from Denys's works are from Colm Luibheid, trans. and ed., *Pseudo-Dionysius: The Complete Works* (New York, 1987)
43 William Wordsworth, 'Lines composed a Few Miles above Tintern Abbey, on Revisiting the Banks of the Wye during a tour. July 13,1798', lines 91–3
44 Ibid., 93–102
45 Wordsworth, 'Expostulation and Reply', 17–24
46 Wordsworth, 'The Tables Turned', 32

3. The Holiness of Nature

1 Exodus 24:17
2 Isaiah 6

3 Rudolf Otto, *The Idea of the Holy: An Inquiry into the Non-rational Factor in the Idea of the Divine and Its Relation to the Rational*, trans. John W. Harvey (Oxford, 1923), 29–30
4 Exodus 3:1–6. Thorkild Jacobsen, *Treasures of Darkness: A History of Mesopotamian Religion* (New Haven, CT, 1976), 6
5 S. David Sperling, 'Israel's Religion in the Near East', in Arthur Green, ed., *Jewish Spirituality*, 2 vols (London and New York, 1986, 1988), 127–8
6 I Kings 19:11–13
7 Psalm 8
8 Ibid. 104:3–4
9 Ibid. 104:29–30
10 Stephen A. Geller, 'Nature's Answer: The Meaning of the Book of Job in Its Intellectual Context', in Hava Tirosh-Samuelson, ed., *Judaism and Ecology: Created World and Revealed World* (Cambridge, MA, 2002), 109–29
11 I Kings 5:32–4
12 Job 3:4–5
13 Robert Alter, *The Art of Biblical Poetry* (New York, 1985), 94–110
14 Job 38:4, 6–9
15 Ibid. 39:18
16 Ibid. 39:1–18
17 Ibid. 40:18–23
18 Exodus 19:16
19 Geller, 'Nature's Answer', 129

20 J. C. Heesterman, *The Inner Conflict of Tradition: Essays in Indian Ritual, Kingship and Society* (Chicago and London, 1985), 70–2
21 Evagrius of Pontus, *On Prayer*, 67, 71, in G. E. H. Palmer, P. Sherrard and K. Ware, eds and trans., *The Philokalia* (London, 1979)
22 Turner, *Darkness of God*, 12–49, 252–72; Andrew Louth, *Denys the Areopagite* (Wilton, CT, 1989)
23 Denys, *Mystical Theology*, 1033 C

4. Our Broken World

1 Aitereya Brahmana 5.32
2 Jaminiya Brahmana 1.111; Taittiriya Brahmana 1.1.3.5; Pañcavimsha Brahmana 12.11.2; trans. Brian K. Smith, *Reflections, Resemblance, Ritual and Religion* (Oxford, 1992), 58–65
3 Shatapatha Brahmana (SB) 1.1.3.5; Jaminiya Brahmana 1.111; Pañcavimsha Brahmana 24.11.2; trans. Smith, *Reflections*, 58–65
4 SB 10.4.2.2; trans. Mahony, *Artful Universe*, 132
5 SB 7.1.2.9–11; trans. Mahony, *Artful Universe*, 135
6 SB 7.1.2.11; trans. Mahony, *Artful Universe*, 134
7 SB 7.1.2.7–8; trans. Mahony, *Artful Universe*, 134
8 Smith, *Reflections*, 65
9 Pañcavimsha Brahmana 18.3
10 Qur'an 19:58, 39:23, 5:83; trans. M. A. S. Abdel Haleem, *The Qur'an: A New Translation* (Oxford, 2010)

11 Suzanne Langer, *Philosophy in a New Key: A Study in the Symbolism of Music, Rite and Art* (Cambridge, MA, 1942), 222
12 Kristina Nelson, *The Art of Reciting the Qur'an* (Cairo, 2001), 99
13 Iain McGilchrist, *The Master and His Emissary: The Divided Brain and the Making of the Western World* (New Haven and London, 2009), 73–4
14 Ibid., 409–10
15 Izutsu, *Sufism and Taoism*, 116–38, 152–4
16 Henry Corbin, *Alone with The Alone: Creative Imagination in the Sūfism of Ibn 'Arabī* (Princeton, NJ, 1969), 184–7
17 Ibid., 185
18 Qur'an 7.156; trans. Arthur J. Arberry, *The Koran Interpreted* (Oxford, 1964)
19 Gershom Scholem, *The Messianic Idea in Judaism and Other Essays on Jewish Spirituality* (New York, 1971), 43–8
20 According to reports by the Organization for Economic Cooperation and Development (OECD) and the Pew Research Center

5. Sacrifice

1 Smith, *Reflections*, 30–4, 72–81
2 Henri Hubert and Marcel Mauss, *Sacrifice: Its Nature and Function*, trans. W. D. Halls (Chicago, 1964), 19–49
3 Smith, *Reflections*, 103; Louis Renou, *Religions of Ancient India* (London, 1953), 18

4 SB 11.2, 2.5; trans. Smith, *Reflections*, 103
5 RV 10.90; trans. Doniger, *Rig Veda*
6 SB 92–3; trans. Mahony, *Artful Universe*
7 Taittiriya Aranyaka 2.10; trans. Mahony, *Artful Universe*
8 Laws of Manu 3.92–3; trans. Mahony, *Artful Universe*
9 Taittiriya Upanishad 1.11.2, 3.10.1; trans. Mahony, *Artful Universe*

6. Kenosis

1 Frederick F. Mote, *The Intellectual Foundations of China* (New York, 1979), 17–18
2 DDJ 52
3 Ibid. 51
4 Ibid. 22
5 Samyutta Nikaya 22.59; trans. Bhikkhu Ñanamoli, *The Life of the Buddha* (Kandy, 1992), 67
6 Philippians 2:6–7
7 Ibid. 2:5
8 Ibid. 2:2–4
9 I Corinthians 13:4
10 Matthew 5:47–8
11 Toshihiko Izutsu, *God and Man in the Koran: Semantics of the Koranic Weltanschauung* (Tokyo, 1964), 148
12 Qur'an 96; trans. Michael Sells, *Approaching the Qur'an: The Early Revelations* (Ashland, OR, 1999)
13 *The Book of Zhuangzi,* trans. David Hinton, *Chuangzu: The Inner Chapters* (Washington, DC, 1998)

7. Gratitude

1 Unless otherwise stated, quotations from the Qur'an are from M. A. S. Abdel Haleem, *The Qur'ān: A New Translation* (Oxford and New York, 2004)
2 Ibrahim Özdemir, 'Toward an Understanding of Environmental Ethics from a Qur'anic Perspective', in Richard C. Foltz, Frederick M. Denny and Azizan Baharuddin, eds, *Islam and Ecology: A Bestowed Trust* (Cambridge, MA, 2003), 7–10
3 Qur'an 80:24–32
4 Sells, *Approaching the Qur'an*, xvi
5 Qur'an 2:115
6 Ibid. 10:6
7 S. H. Nasr, 'The Cosmos and the Natural Order', in Sayyed Hossain Nasr, ed., *Islamic Spirituality: Foundations* (New York, 1987), 347
8 Qur'an 22:18
9 Ibid. 6:95; trans. Arberry, *The Koran Interpreted*
10 Ibid. 6:95–6; trans., Arberry, *The Koran Interpreted*
11 Ibid. 36:38–40
12 Ibid. 55:1–12; trans. Arberry, *The Koran Interpreted*
13 Ibid. 99:6–9; trans. Sells, *Approaching the Qur'an*
14 Ibid. 90:13–16; trans. Sells, *Approaching the Qur'an*
15 Ibid. 88:17–20; trans. Sells, *Approaching the Qur'an*
16 Francis of Assisi, 'Canticle of the Sun', written in Old Italian, 1224; trans. Franciscan Friars, Third Order Regular, Wikipedia

17 Gerard Manley Hopkins, 'Spring', in *Poems of Gerard Manley Hopkins*, ed. Robert Bridges (London, New York and Toronto, 3rd edn, 1952), 71
18 Ibid., 95
19 Mary Oliver, 'The Country of the Trees', in *Blue Horses* (London, 2018)
20 Oliver, 'Do Stones Feel?', in ibid.
21 Amos 1:9,11; 2:7
22 Ibid. 6:4–6
23 Isaiah 1:17–19
24 Luke 6:22–5

8. The Golden Rule

1 Analects 12.3; trans. T. R. Slingerland, *Confucius: Analects* (Indianapolis and Cambridge, 2003)
2 Ibid. 4.15; trans. Slingerland, *Confucius*
3 Ibid. 12.2; trans. Slingerland, *Confucius*
4 Ibid. 6.28; trans. Arthur Waley, *The Analects of Confucius* (New York, 1992)
5 Ibid. 15.23; trans. Waley, *The Analects*
6 Herbert Fingarette, *Confucius: The Secular as Sacred* (New York, 1972), 55–6
7 *Hamlet*, Act 3, Scene 4, l. 150
8 Mencius 2A.2; trans. D. C. Lau, *Mencius* (London, 1970)
9 Ibid. 7A.4; trans. Lau, *Mencius*
10 'The Great Learning (*Daxue*)', trans. Irene Bloom, in William Theodore de Bary and Irene Bloom, eds,

Sources of Chinese Tradition: From Earliest Times to 1600 (New York, 1999), 330–1

11 Irene Bloom, 'The Mean (*Zhongyong*)', in ibid., 333–4

12 Mean 30, in Wing Tsit Chan, ed. and trans., *A Sourcebook of Chinese Philosophy* (Princeton, NJ, 1969), 111–12

13 Ibid. 30, in Chan, *Sourcebook*, 107–8

14 Ibid. 20, in Chan, *Sourcebook*, 107

15 Ibid. 20, in Chan, *Sourcebook*, 108

16 Ibid. 25, in Chan, *Sourcebook*, 109

17 Ibid. 26, in Chan, *Sourcebook*, 110

18 Mean 15.1; trans. Tu Weiming, *Centrality and Commonality: An Essay on Confucian Religiousness* (Albany, NY, 1989)

19 Mean 12.2; in Chan, *Sourcebook*, 100

20 Wing-tsit Chan, trans. and ed., *Reflections on Things at Hand: The Neo-Confucian Anthology Compiled by Chu His and Lü Tsu Ch'ien* (New York and London, 1967), 14.18, 302

21 William Theodore de Bary, Wing-tsit Chan and Burton Watson, eds, *Sources of Chinese Tradition* (New York, 1960), 559

22 Rodney L. Taylor, *The Religious Dimensions of Confucianism* (Albany, NY, 1990), 43–7

23 Chan, *Reflections*, 2.83, 74–5

24 'Western Inscription (Ximing)', trans. Wing-tsit Chan, in de Bary and Bloom, *Sources of Chinese Tradition,* 683–4

25 Chan, *Reflections*, 14.18, 302

26 William Theodore de Bary, 'Neo-Confucian Cultivation and the Seventeenth Century Enlightenment', in

William Theodore de Bary, *The Unfolding of Neo-Confucianism* (New York and London, 1975), 151–90

27 Xi Zhu, *Literary Remains of the Two Chengs*, 2a, in William Theodore de Bary, *Learning for Oneself: Essays on the Individual in Neo-Confucian Thought* (New York, 1991), 283

28 Ibid., 3.31

29 A. C. Graham, *Two Chinese Philosophers: The Metaphysics of the Brothers Ch'eng* (La Salle, IL, 1992), 76

30 Chan, *Reflections*

31 Ibid., 14.25, 291

32 Ibid., 14.4a, 301

33 Ibid., 14.2b, 299

34 Ibid., 2/2ab, 40

35 Ibid., citing Zhu Xi , 99.28a

36 Ibid., 114.2.5, 291

37 Xunzi, 'Dispelling Obsession', in Burton Watson, trans. and ed., *Xunzi: Basic Writings* (New York, 2003), 127–8

38 Daodejing 13, trans. Irene Bloom, in de Bary and Bloom, eds, *Sources of Chinese Tradition*, 83–4

39 Luke 6:27–37

9. Ahimsa

1 Paul Dundas, *The Jains* (2nd edn, London and New York, 2002), 28–30

2 Ibid., 106–7

3 Acaranga Sutra 1.4.111-2, in Dundas, *The Jains*, 41–2

4 Ibid., 1.2.3, in Dundas, *The Jains*

5 Avashyak Sutra 32, in Dundas, *The Jains*, 171
6 Acaranga Sutra 13.115.22; trans. Christopher Key Chapple, *Nonviolence to Animals, Earth and Self in Asian Traditions* (Albany, NY, 1993), 17
7 Yoga Sutra 2.35.
8 Acaranga Sutra 1.1.2.1.5.5; trans. Nathmal Tatia, *Studies in Jaina Philosophy* (Banaras, 1951), 18
9 Patrick Olivelle, ed., *Asoka: In History and Historical Memory* (Delhi, 2009), 1, 254–5
10 Chapple, *Nonviolence*, 18; Abdul Fazl, *Akbar Nama*, trans. H. Beveridge (Calcutta, 1897), 333–4
11 Chapple, *Nonviolence*, 19.
12 Mahabharata 114:5–10; trans. Chapple, *Nonviolence*, 79–80
13 Laurence Sterne, *The Life and Opinions of Tristram Shandy*, Vol. II, Ch. 12

10. Concentric Circles

1 *Shujing* 1; trans. Burton Watson, in de Bary and Bloom, eds, *Sources of Chinese Tradition*, 29.
2 Edward Conze, *Buddhism: Its Essence and Development* (Oxford, 1957), 102
3 Anguttara Nikaya 8.7.3; Richard Gombrich, *How Buddhism Began: The Conditioned Genesis of the Early Teachings* (London and Atlantic Highlands, NJ, 1996), 60–1
4 Anguttara Nikaya 3.65
5 Sutta-Nipata, 118

6 Tu Weiming, 'Beyond Enlightenment Mentality', in Mary Evelyn Tucker and John Berthrong, eds, *Confucianism and Ecology: The Interrelation of Heaven, Earth and Human* (Cambridge, MA, 1998)
7 Wang Yangming, 'Inquiry on the Great Learning', in Chan, *Sourcebook*, 659–60

Epilogue

1 William Wordsworth, 'Lines Composed a Few Miles Above Tintern Abbey', ll. 41, 47–9
2 Samuel Taylor Coleridge, 'Frost at Midnight', ll. 1–2
3 Ibid., ll. 9–10
4 Ibid., ll. 54–5, 59–64
5 Coleridge, 'The Eolian Harp'
6 Coleridge, 'The Rime of the Ancient Mariner', ll. 1–4
7 Ibid., ll. 81–2
8 Ibid., ll. 101–2
9 Ibid., l. 135
10 Ibid., ll. 125–6
11 Ibid., l. 223
12 Ibid., ll. 244–7
13 Ibid.
14 Ibid., ll. 274–87
15 Ibid., l. 291
16 Ibid., ll. 363–72
17 Ibid., ll. 603–6
18 Ibid., ll. 612–17
19 Ibid., ll. 622–5

Select Bibliography

ABRAM, David, *The Spell of the Sensuous: Perception and Language in a More-Than-Human World* (New York, 1996)

ABRAMS, M. H., *Natural Supernaturalism, Tradition and Revolution in Romantic Literature* (New York and London, 1971)

ADDIS, Stephen, and Stanley LOMBARDO, trans., *Tao Te Ching* (Indianapolis, 1993)

ASSMAN, Jan, *The Search for God in Ancient Egypt*, trans. David Lorton (Ithaca and London, 2001)

BELLAH, Robert N., *Religion in Human Evolution: From the Palaeolithic to the Axial Age* (Cambridge, MA, and London, 2011)

BIESE, A., *The Development and the Feeling for Nature in the Middle Ages and Modern Times* (Stockbridge, MA, 1905)

CHAPPLE, Christopher Key, *Nonviolence to Animals, Earth and Self in Asian Traditions* (Albany, NY, 1993)

——— *Hinduism and Ecology: The Intersection of Earth, Sky and Water* (Cambridge, MA, 2000)

——— ed., *Jainism and Ecology: Nonviolence in the Web of Life* (Cambridge, MA, 2002)

CHITTICK, William C., *The Self-Disclosure of God: Principles of Ibn al-'Arabi's Cosmology* (Albany, NY, 1998)

——— *The Sufi Path of Knowledge: Ibn al-'Arabi's Metaphysics of Imagination* (Albany, NY, 1989)

CHODKIEWICZ, Michel, *An Ocean Without a Shore: Ibn Arabi, The Book and the Law* (Albany, NY, 1993)

CORBIN, Henry, *Alone with The Alone: Creative Imagination in the Sufism of Ibn 'Arabi* (Princeton, NJ, 1969)

DE BARY, William Theodore, ed., *The Unfolding of Neo-Confucianism* (New York and London, 1975)

——— *Learning for One's Self: Essays on the Individual in Neo-Confucian Thought* (New York, 1991)

——— ed., *The Buddhist Tradition in India, China and Japan* (New York, 1969)

——— *Self and Society in Ming Thought* (New York, 1970)

——— ed. with Irene Bloom, *Sources of Chinese Tradition* (New York, 1994)

DELLA DORA, Veronica, *Landscape, Nature and the Sacred in Byzantium* (Cambridge, 2016)

DONIGER, Wendy, *The Hindus: An Alternative History* (Oxford, 2008)

——— trans., *The Rig Veda* (London and New York, 1982)

——— ed., *Purana Perennis: Reciprocity and Transformation in Hindu and Jaina Texts* (Albany, NY, 1993)

ELIADE, Mircea, *The Sacred and the Profane*, trans. Willard B. Trask (New York, 1959)

——— *The Myth of the Eternal Return: Or, Cosmos and History*, trans. Willard B. Trask (Princeton, NJ, 1965)

ENO, Robert, *The Confucian Creation of Heaven: Philosophy and the Defense of Ritual Mastery* (Albany, NY, 1990)

FAIRBANK, John King, and Merle GOLDMAN, *China: A New History*, 2nd edn (Cambridge, MA and London, 2006)

FALKENHAUSEN, Lothar von, *Chinese Society in the Age of Confucius (1000–250 BCE)* (Los Angeles, 2006)

FINGARETTE, Herbert, *Confucius: The Secular as Sacred* (New York, 1972)

——— 'The Problem of the Self in the Analects', *Philosophy East and West*, 29.2, 1979

FISHER, CHARLES S., *Meditation in the Wild: Buddhism's Origin in the Heart of Nature*, (Winchester, UK, and Washington, DC, 2013)

FOLTZ, Richard C., Frederick M. DENNY and Azizan BAHARUDDIN, eds, *Islam and Ecology: A Bestowed Trust* (Cambridge, MA, 2003)

FUNG, Yu-Lan, *A Short History of Chinese Philosophy*, ed. Derk Bodde (New York and London, 1976)

GIBSON, James, *The Ecological Approach to Perception* (Boston, 1979)

GIRADOT, N. J., James MILLER and LIU Xiaogan, eds, *Daoism and Ecology: Ways Within a Cosmic Landscape* (Cambridge, MA, 2001)

GONDA, Jan, *Notes on Brahman* (Utrecht, 1950)

——— *The Vision of the Vedic Poets* (Berlin, 1963)

——— *Loka: World and Heaven in the Veda* (Amsterdam, 1966)

——— *Vedic Literature* (Wiesbaden, 1975)

GRAHAM, A. C., *Disputers of the Tao: Philosophical Argument in Ancient China* (La Salle, IL, 1989)

GRAHAM, D. W., ed., *Studies in Greek Philosophy, Vol. 1: The Presocratics* (Princeton, NJ, 1993)

GRANET, Marcel, *Chinese Civilization*, trans. Kathleen E. Innes and Mabel R. Brailsford (New York, 1930)

——— *The Religion of the Chinese People*, trans. and ed. Maurice Freedman (London, 1977)

——— *Festivals and Songs of Ancient China*, trans. E. D. Edwards (London, 1932)

HALL, David, and Roger T. AMES, *Thinking through Confucius* (Albany, NY, 1987)

HALPERN, Daniel, ed., *On Nature: Nature, Landscape and Natural History* (San Francisco, 1987)

HAN SHAN, *Cold Mountain*, trans. G. Snyder (San Francisco, 1969)

——— *The Collected Songs of Cold Mountain*, trans. Red Piner (Port Townsend, WI, 1983)

HEESTERMAN, J. C., *The Broken World of Sacrifice: An Essay in Ancient Indian Religion* (Chicago, 1993)

——— *The Inner Conflict of Tradition* (Chicago, 1985)

HESCHEL, Abraham Joshua, *Man Is Not Alone* (New York, 1951)

HESSEL, Dieter T, and Rosemary Radford RUETHER, eds, *Christianity and Ecology: Seeking the Well-being of Earth and Humans* (Cambridge, MA, 2000)

IBN ISHAQ, Muhammad, *The Life of Muhammad: A Translation of Ibn Ishaq's Sirat Rasul Allah*, trans. Alfred Guillaume (Oxford, 1955)

IDEL, Moshe, *Kabbalah: New Perspectives* (New Haven and London, 1988)

IZUTSU, Toshihiko, *Ethico-Religious Concepts in the Qur'an* (Montreal, London and Ithaca, NY, 2002)

——— *Sufism and Taoism: A Comparative Study of Key Philosophical Concepts* (Berkeley, Los Angeles and London, 1983)

——— *A Comparative Study of the Key Philosophical Concepts in Sufism and Daoism II* (Tokyo, 1967)

JACOBSEN, Thorkild, *The Treasures of Darkness: A History of Mesopotamian Religion* (New Haven and London, 1976)

JAEGER, Werner, *The Theology of the Early Greek Philosophers* (Oxford, 1947)

KAZA, Stephanie, and Kenneth KRAFT, eds, *Dharma Rain: Sources of Buddhist Environmentalism* (Boston and London, 2000)

LAU, D. C., trans. and ed., *Confucius: The Analects* (Lun Yu) (London, 1979)

——— trans. and ed., *Mencius* (London, 1970)

——— trans. and ed., *Lao-tzu: Tao Te Ching* (London, 1963)

LEGGE, James, trans., *Li Ji: The Book of Rites*, ed. Dai Shing (Beijing and Washington, DC, 2013)

——— trans. *The She King: Or, the Book of Poetry* (Oxford, 1893)

LÉVY-BRUHL, Lucien, *How Natives Think*, trans. Lilian A. Clark (New York, 2015)

LUMHOLTZ, Carl, *Symbolism of the Huichol Indians* (London, 1901)

McDONALD, Barry, ed., *Seeing God Everywhere: Essays on Nature and the Sacred* (Bloomington, IN, 2003)

McGILCHRIST, Iain, *The Master and his Emissary: The Divided Brain and the Making of the Western World* (New Haven and London, 2009)

——— *Ways of Attending: How Our Divided Brain Constructs the World* (London and New York, 2019)

McNELEY, James Kale, *Holy Wind in Navajo Philosophy* (Tucson, 1981)

MAHONY, William K., *The Artful Universe: An Introduction to the Vedic Religious Imagination* (Albany, NY, 1998)

MASPERO, Henri, *China in Antiquity*, trans. Frank A. Kerman Jr., (2nd edn, Folkstone, 1978)

——— *La Taoism (mélanges posthumes sur les religions et l'histoire de la Chine)* (Paris, 1950)

MEYENDORFF, John, *Byzantine Theology: Historical Trends and Doctrinal Themes* (New York, 1974)

NADDAF, Gerard, *The Greek Concept of Nature* (Albany, NY, 2005)

NANAMOLI, Bhikkhu, ed. and trans. *The Life of the Buddha according to the Pali Canon* (Kundy, 1992)

NASR, Seyyed Hossein, *Religion and the Order of Nature* (Oxford and New York, 1998)

——— *The Spiritual and Religious Dimensions of the Environmental Crisis* (London, 1999)

——— ed., *Islamic Spirituality: Foundations* (New York, 1987)

NELSON, Lance E., *Purifying the Earthly Body of God: Religion and Ecology in Hindu India* (Albany, NY, 1998)

NELSON, Stephanie, *God and the Land: The Metaphysics of Farming in Hesiod and Virgil* (Oxford and New York, 1998)

PERL, Eric D., *Theophany: The Neoplatonic Philosophy of Dionysius the Areopagite* (New York, 2007)

——— 'Symbol, Sacrament and Hierarchy in Saint Dionysius the Areopagite', *Greek Orthodox Theological Review*, 39, 1994

——— 'St Gregory Palamas and the Metaphysics of Creation', *Dionysius*, 14, 1990

RAHMAN, Fazlur, *Major Themes of the Qur'an* (2nd edn, Chicago and London, 1980)

RENOU, Louis, *Religions of Ancient India* (London, 1953)

RICOEUR, Paul, *Figuring the Sacred: Religion, Narrative and Imagination*, trans. David Pellauer, ed. Mark I. Wallace (Minneapolis, 1995)

SALLIS, John, *The Figure of Nature: On Greek Origins* (Bloomington, IN, 2016)

SCHWARTZ, Benjamin I., *The World of Thought in Ancient China* (Cambridge, MA, 1985)

SHERRARD, Philip, *Human Image, World Image: The Death and Resurrection of Sacred Cosmology* (Evia, Greece, 1992)

SMITH, Brian A., *Reflections on Ritual, Resemblance and Religion* (Oxford, 2002)

TIROSH-SAMUELSON, Hava, ed., *Judaism and Ecology: Created World and Revealed Word* (Cambridge, MA, 2002)

TU, Weiming, *Centrality and Commonality: An Essay on Confucian Religiousness* (Albany, NY, 1989)

TU, Weiming, and Mary Evelyn TUCKER, eds, *Confucian Spirituality I* (New York, 2003)

——— *Confucian Spirituality II* (New York, 2004)

TUCKER, Mary Evelyn, and John BERTHRONG, eds, *Confucianism and Ecology: The Interrelation of Heaven, Earth and Humans* (Cambridge, MA, 1998)

TUCKER, Mary Evelyn, and Duncan Ryúkan WILLIAMS, eds, *Buddhism and Ecology: The Interconnection of Dharma and Deeds* (Cambridge, MA, 1997)

TURNER, Denys, *The Darkness of God: Negativity and the Sacred* (Cambridge, 1995)

——— *Eros and Allegory: Medieval Exegesis on the Song of Songs* (Milton Keynes, 1995)

WALLACE-HADRILL, D. S., *The Greek Patristic View of Nature* (Manchester and New York, 1968)

WATSON, Burton, ed. and trans., *Hzun-Tzu: Basic Writings* (New York, 1963)

——— ed. and trans., *Xunzi: Basic Writings* (New York, 2003)

——— *The Complete Words of Zhuangzi* (New York, 2013)

WILLIAMS, Paul, *Mahayana Buddhism: The Doctrinal Foundations* (London, 1989)

——— *Buddhist Thought* (London, 2004)

Index

penguin.co.uk/vintage